Business Analytics Demystified

Leveraging Data to Make Informed Business Decisions

ANDREA CROSS

© Copyright 2024 by ANDREA CROSS
All Rights Reserved

The presentation of the information is without contract or any type of guarantee assurance. The trademarks that are used are without any consent, and the publication of the trademark is without permission or backing by the trademark owner. All trademarks and brands within this book are for clarifying purposes only and are the owned by the owners themselves, not affiliated with this document.

Table of Contents

Chapter 1

Introduction to Business Analytics

What is Business Analytics?

Business analytics is a field that combines data analysis, statistical methods, and computer-based models to inform and improve business decision-making. It involves a systematic exploration of an organization's data with an emphasis on statistical analysis. Business analytics is not just about collecting data; it's also about using that data to generate insights, predict outcomes, and optimize processes.

At its core, business analytics seeks to answer essential questions that drive strategic and operational decisions. These questions include understanding what has happened (descriptive analytics), why it happened (diagnostic analytics), what is likely to happen in the future (predictive analytics), and what actions should be taken (prescriptive analytics). Each of these facets plays a critical role in the analytics lifecycle and contributes to a holistic understanding of business operations.

Descriptive analytics focuses on summarizing historical data to identify patterns and trends. This form of analytics uses data aggregation and data mining techniques to provide insights into past performance. For instance, a retailer might use descriptive analytics to understand sales trends over the last quarter, identifying peak periods and underperforming products. This foundation is crucial because it provides a clear picture of the current state of the business, enabling more informed decisions.

Moving beyond descriptive analytics, diagnostic analytics delves deeper to understand the reasons behind past performance. It employs techniques such as drill-down, data discovery, data mining, and correlations to investigate the factors that influence outcomes. For example, if a company experiences a sudden drop in sales, diagnostic analytics can help identify whether the cause was a marketing issue, a supply chain problem, or changes in consumer behavior. This deeper understanding is vital for addressing root causes rather than symptoms.

Predictive analytics uses statistical models and machine learning algorithms to forecast future events based on historical data. By identifying patterns and relationships within the data, predictive analytics can provide organizations with a glimpse into what might happen next. For instance, a financial institution might use predictive analytics to assess the likelihood of loan defaults among its customers. These predictions enable businesses to proactively manage risks and capitalize on opportunities.

Prescriptive analytics goes a step further by recommending actions that can help achieve desired outcomes. It combines data, models, and business rules to suggest optimal strategies. For example, a logistics company might use prescriptive analytics to determine the most efficient routes for its delivery trucks, taking into account factors like traffic, weather, and fuel costs. By providing actionable recommendations, prescriptive analytics helps organizations move from insight to impact.

The evolution of business analytics has been driven by advancements in technology and the growing availability of data. In the past, businesses relied heavily on intuition and experience to make decisions. However, the digital age has ushered in an era where data is abundant and accessible, enabling more data-driven decision-making processes. The rise of big data, cloud computing, and advanced analytical tools has transformed how organizations approach decision-making.

One of the key components of business analytics is data. Data is the raw material that analytics processes and transforms into valuable insights. This data can come from various sources, including internal systems like customer relationship management (CRM) systems, enterprise resource planning (ERP) systems, and external sources such as social media, market research, and public datasets. The diversity of data sources enriches the analytical process, providing a more comprehensive view of the business environment.

Data quality and integrity are crucial for effective business analytics. Poor-quality data can lead to incorrect conclusions and misguided decisions. Ensuring data accuracy, completeness, and timeliness is essential for reliable analytics. Organizations must implement robust data governance practices to maintain data quality, including data validation, cleaning, and regular audits.

Another critical component of business analytics is the tools and technologies used to analyze data. These tools range from simple spreadsheet software to sophisticated analytics platforms that incorporate artificial intelligence and machine learning capabilities. The choice of tools depends on the complexity of the analysis, the volume of data, and the specific needs of the organization. Common tools include Microsoft Excel, SQL databases, R, Python, and specialized analytics software like Tableau, SAS, and IBM SPSS.

The role of the business analyst is pivotal in the analytics process. Business analysts act as intermediaries between the data and business stakeholders. They possess a unique blend of technical skills, business acumen, and communication abilities. Their primary responsibility is to translate business requirements into analytical tasks and interpret the results of data analysis into actionable insights. Effective communication is essential, as analysts must convey complex analytical findings in a manner that is understandable to non-technical stakeholders.

One of the challenges in business analytics is dealing with common misconceptions. Some businesses view analytics as a magic solution that will automatically solve their problems. However, analytics is a tool that requires proper implementation and interpretation. Without a clear understanding of business objectives and the context in which data exists, analytics can lead to misleading conclusions. Another misconception is that more data always leads to better insights. In reality, the quality of data and the relevance of the analysis are far more important than the sheer volume of data.

Ethical considerations also play a significant role in business analytics. As organizations collect and analyze increasing amounts of data, they must ensure that they respect privacy and comply with regulations such as the General Data Protection Regulation (GDPR). Ethical analytics practices include obtaining informed consent from data subjects, anonymizing sensitive information, and being transparent about data usage. Organizations must balance the potential benefits of analytics with the responsibility to protect individual privacy and prevent misuse of data.

Despite these challenges, the benefits of business analytics are substantial. Organizations that effectively leverage analytics can gain a competitive edge by making more informed decisions, identifying new opportunities, and optimizing operations. Analytics can lead to improved customer experiences, increased efficiency, and higher profitability. For instance, retailers can use analytics to personalize marketing efforts, manufacturers can optimize production processes, and healthcare providers can enhance patient care.

In conclusion, business analytics is a powerful tool that transforms data into actionable insights, driving better decision-making across various business functions. By understanding what business analytics is, its key components, and the different types of analytics, organizations can harness the power of data to achieve their strategic objectives. As technology continues to evolve and data becomes even more integral to business operations, the importance of analytics will only continue to grow, shaping the future of how businesses operate and compete in the marketplace.

To fully capitalize on the potential of business analytics, it's essential for organizations to foster a data-driven culture. A data-driven culture prioritizes evidence-based decision-making and encourages employees at all levels to use data as a critical component of their daily work. This cultural shift often requires significant changes in mindset, processes, and organizational structure.

The Evolution of Business Analytics

The story of business analytics is as much about technological advancement as it is about the shifting paradigms in how businesses approach decision-making. To understand the current state of business analytics, it's essential to trace its evolution from its early beginnings to the sophisticated systems we use today.

In the early days of business, decisions were often made based on gut feelings, personal experience, and limited data. Businesses relied on basic accounting records and rudimentary statistical methods. The data available was scarce and often outdated by the time it was analyzed. The introduction of computers in the mid-20th century, however, marked the beginning of a new era. Companies started using mainframe computers to process data faster and more accurately than manual methods allowed. This period saw the birth of Management Information Systems (MIS), which provided managers with reports and summaries of the organization's operations.

The 1970s and 1980s witnessed significant advancements in database technologies. Relational databases emerged, allowing for more efficient data storage and retrieval. Structured Query Language (SQL) became the standard for managing and manipulating data, making it easier for businesses to extract meaningful information from their databases. During this time, the concept of Decision Support Systems (DSS) gained traction. DSS were interactive software-based systems designed to help decision-makers compile useful information from raw data, documents, and personal knowledge.

The 1990s brought the rise of Enterprise Resource Planning (ERP) systems, which integrated various business processes into a single unified system. ERPs centralized data from different departments within an organization, such as finance, human resources, and supply chain management. This integration facilitated better data flow, making it easier for businesses to get a comprehensive view of their operations. Alongside ERP systems, the development of Online Analytical Processing (OLAP) tools allowed for more sophisticated data analysis. OLAP enabled multi-dimensional analysis of data, providing deeper insights into business performance.

The turn of the millennium marked the beginning of the big data era. The proliferation of the internet, social media, and mobile devices generated vast amounts of data. Traditional data processing tools were not equipped to handle the volume, variety, and velocity of this data. This challenge gave rise to new technologies such as Hadoop and NoSQL databases, which could efficiently process and store large datasets. Businesses began to realize the potential of big data to uncover patterns, trends, and correlations that were previously hidden.

With the explosion of data came the need for more advanced analytical techniques. Predictive analytics emerged as a powerful tool, allowing businesses to anticipate future events based on historical data. Techniques such as regression analysis, time series analysis, and machine learning algorithms enabled more accurate forecasting and risk assessment. For example, retailers could predict inventory needs, financial institutions could assess credit risk, and manufacturers could predict equipment failures.

The evolution of business analytics also saw the rise of data visualization tools. Visualization tools like Tableau, Power BI, and QlikView revolutionized how businesses interact with data. These tools made it possible to create interactive and intuitive dashboards, enabling users to explore data visually and gain insights quickly. Visualization helps bridge the gap between complex data and decision-makers, making it easier to understand and act upon analytical findings.

In recent years, real-time analytics has become increasingly important. The ability to analyze data as it is generated provides businesses with immediate insights, allowing for faster decision-making. For instance, e-commerce platforms can adjust pricing dynamically based on real-time demand, and financial markets can detect and respond to fraudulent activities almost instantaneously. Real-time analytics is powered by advancements in data streaming technologies and in-memory computing, which allow for rapid processing of large datasets.

The evolution of business analytics is also characterized by the increasing democratization of data. In the past, data analysis was primarily the domain of specialized data scientists and analysts. Today, self-service analytics tools empower non-technical users to perform their own analyses. This shift has been driven by the development of user-friendly interfaces and the integration of natural language processing capabilities, which allow users to interact with data using everyday language.

As business analytics continues to evolve, several trends are shaping its future. One such trend is the emphasis on data governance and ethics. As organizations collect more data, they must ensure that it is used responsibly and ethically. This includes protecting data privacy, ensuring data accuracy, and being transparent about how data is used. Regulatory frameworks such as the General Data Protection Regulation (GDPR) in Europe highlight the importance of data governance in today's data-driven world.

Another trend is the integration of advanced analytics into business processes. Instead of being a standalone function, analytics is increasingly embedded into business workflows. This integration allows for continuous monitoring and optimization of processes, leading to more agile and responsive organizations. For example, supply chain analytics can be integrated into logistics operations to optimize routes and reduce costs in real time.

Moreover, the role of analytics in driving innovation cannot be overstated. Businesses are leveraging analytics to identify new market opportunities, develop innovative products, and enhance customer experiences. For instance, companies use sentiment analysis to gauge customer opinions and tailor their products and services accordingly. Analytics-driven innovation helps businesses stay competitive in a rapidly changing market.

The evolution of business analytics is a testament to the transformative power of data. From the early days of manual record-keeping to the sophisticated analytical tools of today, the journey has been marked by continuous innovation and adaptation. As businesses navigate an increasingly complex and data-rich landscape, the ability to harness the power of analytics will be a key differentiator. Organizations that embrace analytics as a strategic asset will be better positioned to make informed decisions, drive innovation, and achieve sustainable growth.

In conclusion, the evolution of business analytics reflects the broader trends in technology and business strategy. By understanding this evolution, businesses can appreciate the value of analytics and its potential to drive better decision-making. As data continues to grow in volume and complexity, the future of business analytics holds exciting possibilities for those willing to invest in its capabilities. The journey of business analytics is far from over, and its ongoing evolution will continue to shape the way businesses operate and compete in the years to come.

As we gaze into the future of business analytics, several emerging trends and technologies promise to further revolutionize the field. One such trend is the increasing importance of augmented analytics. Augmented analytics leverages machine learning and artificial intelligence to automate data preparation, insight discovery, and sharing. This approach not only accelerates the analytics process but also makes it more accessible to non-experts, enabling a broader range of employees to derive actionable insights from complex data sets.

Importance of Data-Driven Decision Making

In today's business landscape, data-driven decision-making has become a cornerstone of successful organizations. Unlike traditional decision-making, which often relies on intuition or past experiences, data-driven decision-making leverages factual data to guide business strategies and operational choices. This approach not only enhances accuracy but also provides a competitive edge, enabling companies to navigate complex markets with confidence and agility.

At its core, data-driven decision-making involves collecting relevant data, analyzing it to extract actionable insights, and using those insights to inform decisions. This process begins with identifying the key metrics that align with the organization's goals. These metrics, often referred to as Key Performance Indicators (KPIs), provide a quantifiable measure of performance and progress. By tracking KPIs, businesses can monitor their health and identify areas for improvement.

One of the primary advantages of data-driven decision-making is improved accuracy. Decisions based on data are grounded in reality and evidence, reducing the risk of errors that can arise from guesswork or biases. For example, a retail company analyzing sales data can identify which products are performing well and which are not. This insight allows them to make informed decisions about inventory management, marketing strategies, and product development, ultimately leading to better financial outcomes.

Moreover, data-driven decision-making fosters a culture of accountability and transparency within organizations. When decisions are backed by data, it becomes easier to justify and communicate those decisions to stakeholders. This transparency builds trust and ensures that everyone in the organization understands the rationale behind strategic choices. For instance, if a company decides to allocate more budget to digital marketing based on data showing higher returns on investment compared to traditional advertising, employees and stakeholders are more likely to support that decision.

Another significant benefit of data-driven decision-making is its ability to uncover hidden patterns and trends. Advanced analytical techniques, such as data mining and predictive analytics, can reveal insights that might not be immediately apparent. For instance, a financial institution can analyze customer transaction data to identify patterns indicative of fraudulent activity. By proactively addressing these patterns, the institution can prevent fraud and protect its customers.

Data-driven decision-making also enhances operational efficiency. By analyzing data related to business processes, companies can identify bottlenecks, streamline operations, and reduce costs. For example, a manufacturing company might use data analytics to monitor production line performance. By identifying inefficiencies and making data-informed adjustments, they can increase productivity and reduce waste.

Furthermore, this approach enables businesses to be more responsive to market changes. In a rapidly evolving market, having access to real-time data allows companies to pivot quickly and adapt their strategies. For example, during the COVID-19 pandemic, many businesses used data to track shifts in consumer behavior and adjust their offerings accordingly. Restaurants, for instance, leveraged data to understand the surge in demand for delivery services and adapted their operations to meet this new demand.

Customer insights are another area where data-driven decision-making proves invaluable. By analyzing customer data, businesses can gain a deeper understanding of their preferences, behaviors, and needs. This information is crucial for developing targeted marketing campaigns, personalized customer experiences, and new product offerings. For example, an e-commerce company can analyze browsing and purchase history to recommend products tailored to individual customers, thus enhancing customer satisfaction and loyalty.

Data-driven decision-making is not without its challenges. One of the primary obstacles is ensuring data quality. Inaccurate or incomplete data can lead to flawed insights and poor decisions. Therefore, businesses must invest in robust data management practices, including data cleaning and validation, to maintain the integrity of their data. Additionally, organizations must address data silos, where information is isolated within different departments. Integrating data across the organization ensures a comprehensive view and more informed decision-making.

Another challenge is building the necessary analytical capabilities within the organization. This involves not only investing in the right tools and technologies but also developing the skills required to analyze and interpret data. Businesses should provide training and resources to employees, fostering a data-literate workforce capable of leveraging data effectively. Moreover, hiring data analysts or partnering with external experts can help bridge any skill gaps.

Despite these challenges, the benefits of data-driven decision-making far outweigh the obstacles. To successfully implement this approach, businesses should start by establishing a clear data strategy. This strategy should outline the goals, data sources, analytical methods, and tools required to support data-driven decision-making. It should also define the roles and responsibilities of individuals involved in the process, ensuring accountability and coordination.

Furthermore, businesses should foster a data-driven culture. This involves promoting the value of data at all levels of the organization and encouraging employees to use data in their everyday decision-making. Leaders play a crucial role in setting the tone and leading by example. By consistently making data-backed decisions and celebrating data-driven successes, leaders can inspire others to follow suit.

Technology also plays a vital role in enabling data-driven decision-making. Businesses should invest in advanced analytics tools, data visualization software, and cloud-based platforms that facilitate data access and analysis. These technologies make it easier to process large volumes of data, generate insights, and share findings across the organization. For example, data visualization tools can transform complex datasets into intuitive charts and graphs, making insights more accessible and understandable.

Finally, businesses should continuously monitor and evaluate the effectiveness of their data-driven decision-making processes. This involves regularly reviewing the data strategy, assessing the quality of data, and measuring the impact of data-driven decisions on business outcomes. By doing so, organizations can identify areas for improvement and ensure that their data-driven initiatives remain aligned with their strategic goals.

In conclusion, data-driven decision-making is a powerful approach that can significantly enhance business performance. By leveraging data to inform decisions, organizations can improve accuracy, uncover hidden insights, increase efficiency, and respond swiftly to market changes. While challenges exist, a clear data strategy, a data-driven culture, and the right technology can help businesses harness the full potential of data-driven decision-making. As the business environment continues to evolve, the ability to make informed, data-backed decisions will remain a critical differentiator for successful organizations.

In the rapidly evolving business landscape, the imperative for data-driven decision-making cannot be overstated. Decision-makers armed with accurate, timely data can pivot strategies, optimize processes, and anticipate trends, ensuring that their organizations remain agile and competitive. However, the journey toward fully embracing data-driven decision-making is multifaceted, requiring a concerted effort across various organizational dimensions.

Key Components of Business Analytics

Business analytics has emerged as a pivotal tool for organizations seeking to harness the power of data to make informed decisions, optimize operations, and gain a competitive edge. At its essence, business analytics involves the systematic analysis of data to uncover patterns, derive insights, and support decision-making processes. Understanding the key components of business analytics is crucial for any organization aiming to leverage data effectively.

The first and most fundamental component of business analytics is data collection. High-quality data is the bedrock upon which all analytics efforts are built. Data can be sourced from various channels, including transactional databases, customer feedback, social media, sensors, and more. Ensuring the accuracy, completeness, and relevance of this data is paramount. Organizations must implement robust data governance practices to maintain data integrity and reliability. This involves establishing protocols for data entry, storage, and security, as well as regular audits to identify and rectify any discrepancies.

Once data is collected, the next critical step is data preprocessing. Raw data often contains noise, missing values, and inconsistencies that must be addressed before analysis. Data preprocessing involves cleaning the data, handling missing values, and transforming it into a suitable format for analysis. Techniques such as normalization, standardization, and data imputation are commonly used to prepare data for subsequent stages. Effective data preprocessing enhances the quality of insights derived from the analysis and ensures that the results are reliable.

Data exploration and visualization are vital components that allow analysts to understand the underlying patterns and trends within the data. Data exploration involves summarizing the data, identifying outliers, and detecting relationships between variables. Visualization tools, such as charts, graphs, and dashboards, play a crucial role in this process by making complex data more accessible and interpretable. For instance, a sales manager can use a line chart to visualize monthly sales trends, helping to identify seasonal patterns and inform inventory planning.

Descriptive analytics is another key component that focuses on summarizing historical data to understand what has happened in the past. This type of analysis provides a retrospective view of business performance, helping organizations to identify successes and failures. Common techniques in descriptive analytics include statistical measures such as mean, median, mode, and standard deviation, as well as data aggregation methods. For example, a retailer might use descriptive analytics to analyze past sales data and determine which products were the top sellers during a specific period.

Building on descriptive analytics, diagnostic analytics seeks to explain why certain events occurred. This component involves identifying the root causes of observed patterns and trends. Techniques such as correlation analysis, regression analysis, and hypothesis testing are commonly used in diagnostic analytics. By understanding the factors driving business outcomes, organizations can make more informed decisions. For instance, if a company notices a decline in customer satisfaction, diagnostic analytics might reveal that longer delivery times are the primary cause, prompting the company to streamline its logistics processes.

Predictive analytics takes business analytics a step further by using historical data to forecast future outcomes. This component leverages statistical models and machine learning algorithms to predict trends, behaviors, and events. Predictive analytics can help organizations anticipate customer needs, optimize inventory levels, and mitigate risks. For example, a financial institution might use predictive analytics to assess the likelihood of loan defaults based on past borrower behavior, enabling them to make more informed lending decisions.

Prescriptive analytics, the most advanced component, goes beyond prediction to recommend specific actions that can optimize outcomes. This type of analytics uses optimization algorithms, simulation, and decision analysis to suggest the best course of action given certain constraints and objectives. Prescriptive analytics can be particularly valuable in complex decision-making scenarios where multiple factors must be considered. For instance, a supply chain manager might use prescriptive analytics to determine the optimal inventory levels that minimize costs while ensuring product availability.

A critical aspect of business analytics is the selection and use of appropriate tools and technologies. There is a wide range of software and platforms available that cater to different aspects of analytics, from data preprocessing to visualization and advanced analytics. Popular tools include spreadsheet software like Microsoft Excel for basic analysis, data visualization tools like Tableau and Power BI, and statistical software like R and SAS. Additionally, database management systems and data warehousing solutions play a crucial role in storing and managing large volumes of data.

Another essential component is the development of analytical skills and a data-driven culture within the organization. While technology is important, the ability to interpret and act on data insights is equally crucial. Organizations should invest in training programs to enhance the analytical capabilities of their employees. This includes not only technical skills, such as data manipulation and statistical analysis, but also critical thinking and problem-solving skills. Encouraging a culture that values data-driven decision-making can significantly enhance the effectiveness of business analytics initiatives.

Communication and collaboration are also key components in the successful implementation of business analytics. Insights derived from data analysis must be effectively communicated to stakeholders to inform decision-making. This requires clear and concise reporting, often supported by visualizations that highlight key findings. Collaboration between different departments, such as marketing, finance, and operations, ensures that data insights are shared and leveraged across the organization. For example, marketing teams can collaborate with data analysts to refine targeting strategies based on customer behavior data.

Ethical considerations and data privacy are increasingly important components of business analytics. Organizations must ensure that their data collection and analysis practices comply with relevant regulations and ethical standards. This includes obtaining informed consent from individuals, anonymizing sensitive data, and implementing robust security measures to protect data from breaches.

Adhering to ethical guidelines not only protects the organization from legal repercussions but also builds trust with customers and stakeholders.

In conclusion, the key components of business analytics encompass a comprehensive approach to leveraging data for informed decision-making. From data collection and preprocessing to advanced analytics and ethical considerations, each component plays a crucial role in the overall process. By understanding and effectively implementing these components, organizations can unlock the full potential of their data, driving growth, innovation, and competitive advantage. Business analytics is not just a technical endeavor but a strategic imperative that requires a holistic approach and a commitment to continuous improvement.

Incorporating these components into a cohesive business analytics strategy is essential for achieving sustained success. Central to this strategy is a clear alignment of analytics initiatives with the organization's overarching goals and objectives. This alignment ensures that data-driven efforts are not conducted in isolation but are directly contributing to the business's strategic priorities.

Common Misconceptions and Challenges

Navigating the complex terrain of business analytics can be daunting, especially for those new to the field. Misconceptions about what business analytics entails and the challenges it presents can hinder progress and result in suboptimal outcomes. Understanding these common pitfalls is essential for anyone aiming to leverage data effectively within their organization.

A prevalent misconception is that business analytics is solely about technology. While software and analytical tools are indeed a crucial part of the process, business analytics is fundamentally about decision-making. The technology serves as a means to an end, providing the data and insights needed to inform strategic choices. However, without a clear understanding of the business context and objectives, even the most advanced tools can fail to deliver meaningful results. Therefore, it's vital to approach analytics with a balanced perspective, recognizing the importance of both technical and business acumen.

Another common misconception is the belief that more data automatically leads to better insights. While having a large volume of data can be advantageous, it is the quality of the data that ultimately matters. Inaccurate, incomplete, or irrelevant data can lead to misleading conclusions and poor decision-making. Organizations must prioritize data quality by implementing rigorous data governance practices, ensuring that data is accurate, consistent, and up to date. This involves regular data audits, validation processes, and the establishment of clear data management protocols.

Many beginners also assume that business analytics is a one-time project rather than an ongoing process. In reality, analytics should be integrated into the daily operations of an organization. It is not enough to analyze data once and expect long-term benefits;

continuous monitoring, analysis, and refinement are necessary to adapt to changing conditions and new information. This iterative approach allows organizations to stay agile and responsive, making data-driven adjustments as needed to achieve their goals.

One of the significant challenges in business analytics is the integration of data from disparate sources. Organizations often collect data from various systems, such as customer relationship management (CRM) platforms, enterprise resource planning (ERP) systems, social media, and more. Combining these datasets into a cohesive whole can be technically challenging and time-consuming. Data integration requires careful planning and the use of appropriate tools and techniques to ensure that data from different sources can be accurately and meaningfully combined. Overcoming this challenge is crucial for obtaining a holistic view of the business and deriving comprehensive insights.

Resistance to change is another significant hurdle. Implementing business analytics often requires changes in processes, roles, and even organizational culture. Employees may be skeptical or fearful of these changes, particularly if they perceive analytics as a threat to their jobs. Effective change management strategies are essential to address these concerns and foster a culture that embraces data-driven decision-making. This includes clear communication about the benefits of analytics, training programs to build analytical skills, and involving employees in the analytics process to gain their buy-in and support.

There is also a misconception that advanced statistical and mathematical skills are required to benefit from business analytics. While having a solid understanding of these areas can be beneficial, it is not a prerequisite for leveraging analytics effectively. Many modern analytics tools are user-friendly and designed for business users with no advanced technical background. These tools often include intuitive interfaces, drag-and-drop functionality, and pre-built models that simplify the analysis process. The key is to focus on the business questions that need to be answered and use the appropriate tools to derive actionable insights.

A significant challenge in business analytics is ensuring data privacy and security. With the increasing volume of data being collected and analyzed, protecting sensitive information has become more critical than ever. Organizations must comply with data privacy regulations and implement robust security measures to safeguard their data. This includes encrypting data, using secure access controls, and regularly monitoring for potential security breaches. Failing to address these issues can result in legal repercussions and damage to the organization's reputation.

Another common misconception is that business analytics can provide definitive answers to all business questions. While analytics can offer valuable insights and predictions, it is not a crystal ball. The results of any analysis are based on the quality of the data and the assumptions underlying the analytical models. Therefore, it is essential to approach analytics with a critical mindset, questioning the results and considering multiple perspectives before making decisions. This critical thinking ensures that insights are interpreted correctly and applied effectively within the business context.

A frequent challenge is the underestimation of the resources required for successful analytics initiatives. Effective business analytics involves not only investing in the right tools and technologies but also dedicating sufficient time, budget, and human resources. Organizations must recognize that building an analytics capability is a strategic investment that requires ongoing support and commitment. This includes hiring skilled analysts, providing continuous training, and allocating budget for analytics projects. Underestimating these requirements can lead to incomplete or unsuccessful analytics initiatives.

Another misconception is that business analytics is only for large organizations with vast resources. In reality, businesses of all sizes can benefit from analytics. Small and medium-sized enterprises (SMEs) can leverage analytics to gain insights into their operations, understand customer behavior, and identify growth opportunities. Many analytics tools are scalable and offer pricing models that cater to smaller businesses. By starting small and gradually building their analytics capabilities, SMEs can achieve significant benefits without overwhelming their resources.

One of the most significant challenges is bridging the gap between data scientists and business leaders. Data scientists possess the technical expertise to analyze data, while business leaders have the strategic vision to make decisions. However, these two groups often speak different languages and may struggle to communicate effectively. Bridging this gap requires fostering collaboration and mutual understanding. Data scientists should strive to present their findings in a clear, business-oriented manner, while business leaders should seek to understand the basics of analytics to engage in informed discussions. This collaboration ensures that analytical insights are aligned with business goals and can be translated into actionable strategies.

In conclusion, understanding the common misconceptions and challenges in business analytics is crucial for successfully navigating this complex field. By recognizing that analytics is not just about technology, prioritizing data quality, integrating data from various sources, managing change effectively, and addressing data privacy and security concerns, organizations can overcome these hurdles. Additionally, fostering a culture of continuous learning, investing in the necessary resources, and bridging the communication gap between data scientists and business leaders are essential for maximizing the value of analytics. Business analytics, when approached with the right mindset and strategies, can drive significant improvements in decision-making, operational efficiency, and overall business performance.

Embracing business analytics is an ongoing journey that requires dedication, adaptability, and strategic thinking. As organizations embark on this journey, they must be prepared to face and overcome various obstacles.

Chapter 2

Data Collection and Management

Types of Data: Structured and Unstructured

Data is the lifeblood of modern business operations, driving decisions, strategies, and innovations. Understanding the types of data available—structured and unstructured—is essential for harnessing its potential. Each type of data has unique characteristics, benefits, and challenges, and knowing how to manage and analyze them effectively can significantly impact an organization's success.

Structured data is highly organized and easily searchable, typically stored in databases and spreadsheets. Think of data in rows and columns, where each piece of information fits neatly into predefined categories. Common examples include transaction records, customer information, and inventory data. This data type follows a consistent format, making it straightforward to input, search, and analyze using traditional data management tools and techniques.

One of the main advantages of structured data is its ease of use. Because it adheres to a strict schema, structured data can be quickly queried and processed using SQL (Structured Query Language) and other database management systems. This predictability allows for efficient storage, retrieval, and analysis, enabling businesses to generate reports, track performance metrics, and uncover trends with relative ease. For instance, a retail company might use structured data to analyze sales patterns and optimize inventory levels.

However, the rigidity of structured data can also be a limitation. Its fixed format means it cannot easily accommodate the complexity and variability of real-world information. As businesses expand and diversify, they often encounter data that doesn't fit neatly into predefined categories. This is where unstructured data comes into play.

Unstructured data, in contrast, lacks a predefined format or organization, making it more challenging to analyze but also more reflective of the complexity of real-world information. Examples of unstructured data include emails, social media posts, videos, images, and audio recordings. This type of data is rich in information and can provide deep insights into customer behavior, preferences, and trends that structured data might miss.

While unstructured data offers a wealth of opportunities, it also presents significant challenges. The lack of a consistent format makes it difficult to store, search, and analyze using traditional database systems. Advanced techniques such as natural language processing (NLP), machine learning (ML), and big data analytics are often required to extract meaningful insights from unstructured data. For example, sentiment analysis tools can analyze social media posts to gauge public opinion about a brand, while image recognition software can categorize and tag photos based on their content.

The integration of structured and unstructured data can lead to a more comprehensive understanding of business operations and customer interactions. By combining these two data types, organizations can create a richer, more nuanced picture of their environment. For instance, a company might analyze structured sales data alongside unstructured customer feedback from social media to identify not only what products are selling well but also why customers like or dislike them.

Achieving this integration requires a robust data strategy and the right technological infrastructure. Data lakes, which store vast amounts of raw data in its native format, are one approach to managing both structured and unstructured data. By using data lakes, organizations can collect and store data from various sources without worrying about format constraints. Advanced analytics tools can then process and analyze this data to uncover valuable insights.

Another critical aspect of managing both types of data is data governance. Establishing clear policies and procedures for data collection, storage, and analysis ensures data quality, security, and compliance with regulations. This is particularly important when dealing with unstructured data, which can contain sensitive information that must be handled with care.

Data quality is a crucial consideration for both structured and unstructured data. Inaccurate or incomplete data can lead to erroneous conclusions and poor decision-making. Implementing data validation and cleaning processes helps maintain data integrity. For structured data, this might involve regular audits and consistency checks, while for unstructured data, techniques such as text normalization and entity recognition can improve data quality.

Security is another vital concern. Structured data is often stored in centralized databases, making it easier to protect using traditional security measures such as encryption and access controls. Unstructured data, however, is more dispersed and can reside in various formats and locations, posing additional security challenges. Organizations must implement comprehensive security strategies that address both structured and unstructured data, ensuring that sensitive information remains protected from unauthorized access and breaches.

Compliance with data protection regulations, such as the General Data Protection Regulation (GDPR) and the California Consumer Privacy Act (CCPA), is essential for all types of data. These regulations impose strict requirements on how organizations collect, store, and process personal data. Ensuring compliance involves not only adhering to legal standards but also fostering a culture of data responsibility within the organization. This includes training employees on data privacy practices and regularly reviewing and updating data policies.

The analysis of structured and unstructured data often requires different skill sets and tools. Data analysts and database administrators typically manage structured data, using SQL and business intelligence (BI) tools to generate reports and dashboards. For unstructured data, data scientists and engineers might employ programming languages like Python and R, along with specialized tools for text analysis, image recognition, and big data processing. Building a diverse team with expertise in both areas is crucial for leveraging the full potential of data.

Visualization is a powerful technique for making sense of both structured and unstructured data. Tools like Tableau, Power BI, and QlikView can create interactive visualizations that help stakeholders understand complex data sets and identify patterns and trends. For unstructured data, visualizations might include word clouds, sentiment graphs, and network diagrams, providing new perspectives on text and social media data.

The future of data management lies in the seamless integration of structured and unstructured data. As technologies evolve, we can expect more sophisticated tools and platforms that simplify the process of combining and analyzing these data types. Innovations in artificial intelligence and machine learning will continue to enhance our ability to extract insights from unstructured data, while advancements in database technologies will improve the efficiency of structured data management.

In conclusion, understanding the distinctions and interplay between structured and unstructured data is fundamental for modern businesses. Structured data offers predictability and ease of use, while unstructured data provides depth and richness. By effectively managing and integrating both types of data, organizations can gain comprehensive insights, make informed decisions, and stay competitive in an increasingly data-driven world. The journey involves addressing challenges related to data quality, security, compliance, and the need for diverse skills and technologies. By embracing these challenges and leveraging the strengths of both structured and unstructured data, businesses can unlock the full potential of their data assets and drive innovation and growth.

One of the most exciting developments in the realm of data is the emergence of hybrid data architectures. These architectures are designed to bridge the gap between structured and unstructured data, enabling businesses to leverage the strengths of both. Hybrid data architectures combine the scalability and flexibility of data lakes with the reliability and performance of traditional data warehouses. This approach allows organizations to store vast amounts of diverse data types while maintaining the ability to quickly query and analyze structured data.

Data Sources and Acquisition Methods

Data sources and acquisition methods form the backbone of any data-driven strategy, influencing the quality, relevance, and timeliness of the insights derived. Understanding where data originates and how to collect it effectively ensures that businesses make informed decisions based on accurate and comprehensive information. This chapter delves into the various data sources available to organizations and explores the methods for acquiring data from these sources.

Data can be broadly categorized into internal and external sources. Internal data originates from within the organization, encompassing information generated through daily operations, transactions, and interactions. Examples include sales records, customer databases, financial statements, and employee performance data. This data is typically structured and readily accessible through internal systems and databases, providing a reliable foundation for analysis.

External data, on the other hand, comes from outside the organization and includes information that can provide additional context or insights when combined with internal data. Examples of external data sources include market research reports, social media platforms, government databases, and third-party data providers. External data can be both structured and unstructured, and acquiring it often requires specific techniques and tools.

One of the most common internal data sources is transactional data, captured from various business processes such as sales, purchases, and inventory management. Transactional data is typically stored in databases and can be easily accessed using query languages like SQL. This data provides a detailed record of business activities, allowing organizations to track performance, identify trends, and make data-driven decisions.

Customer relationship management (CRM) systems are another vital internal data source. CRM systems store information about customer interactions, preferences, and behaviors, offering valuable insights into customer needs and satisfaction. By analyzing CRM data, businesses can tailor their marketing strategies, improve customer service, and foster stronger customer relationships.

Enterprise resource planning (ERP) systems integrate data from various business functions, including finance, human resources, supply chain, and production. ERP systems provide a holistic view of organizational operations, enabling efficient resource management and strategic planning. The data from ERP systems is typically structured and can be readily analyzed to optimize business processes and improve overall performance.

External data sources offer a wealth of information that can complement internal data and provide a broader perspective. Market research reports, for instance, offer insights into industry trends, competitor activities, and consumer preferences. These reports, often produced by specialized research firms, can be purchased or accessed through subscriptions, providing organizations with valuable external benchmarks.

Social media platforms are a rich source of unstructured data, capturing real-time public opinions, trends, and conversations. Businesses can analyze social media data to understand customer sentiment, track brand mentions, and identify emerging trends. Social media data is typically acquired through APIs (Application Programming Interfaces) provided by platforms like Twitter,

Facebook, and Instagram, allowing organizations to collect and analyze large volumes of data.

Government databases and public records provide authoritative and reliable information on various topics, including economic indicators, demographic statistics, and regulatory frameworks. Accessing this data often involves navigating government websites or using APIs provided by government agencies. Public records can offer valuable context for business decisions, such as market entry strategies or compliance requirements.

Third-party data providers offer a wide range of data sets, from consumer behavior and purchasing patterns to weather data and geographic information. These providers collect, curate, and sell data to organizations seeking to enhance their internal data with external insights. Subscribing to third-party data services can help businesses gain a competitive edge by accessing high-quality, up-to-date information.

To effectively acquire data from these diverse sources, organizations must employ a variety of data acquisition methods. Web scraping is a technique used to collect data from websites by extracting information from HTML code. This method is particularly useful for gathering data from public websites, such as competitor pricing, product reviews, or news articles. Web scraping tools and frameworks, such as Beautiful Soup and Scrapy, automate the process, allowing organizations to collect large volumes of data efficiently.

APIs are another powerful tool for data acquisition, providing a standardized way to access data from external sources. APIs allow organizations to connect directly to data providers, retrieve specific information, and integrate it into their systems. For instance, financial data APIs can provide real-time stock prices, while weather APIs offer up-to-date weather forecasts. Using APIs ensures that data is collected accurately and efficiently, often in real-time.

IoT (Internet of Things) devices generate vast amounts of data from sensors and connected devices, offering real-time insights into various environments. For example, manufacturing companies use IoT sensors to monitor equipment performance and predict maintenance needs, while retailers use IoT data to track inventory levels and optimize supply chains. Collecting data from IoT devices requires specialized platforms and protocols to handle the high volume and velocity of data generated.

Surveys and questionnaires are traditional but effective methods for acquiring primary data directly from individuals. These tools allow organizations to gather specific information related to customer satisfaction, employee engagement, or market research. Online survey platforms, such as SurveyMonkey and Google Forms, simplify the process of designing, distributing, and analyzing surveys, making it easier to collect and interpret data.

Mobile data collection leverages the ubiquity of smartphones and mobile devices to gather data from users in various contexts. Mobile apps can collect data on user behavior, location, and interactions, providing valuable insights into customer preferences and habits. For instance, fitness apps track user activity and health metrics, while retail apps monitor shopping behaviors and preferences. Ensuring the privacy and security of mobile data is crucial, requiring adherence to data protection regulations and best practices.

Data acquisition also involves addressing challenges related to data quality, privacy, and security. Ensuring data accuracy and completeness is essential for reliable analysis, requiring robust data validation and cleaning processes. Data privacy regulations, such as GDPR and CCPA, impose strict requirements on how organizations collect, store, and use personal data. Compliance with these regulations involves implementing data protection measures, obtaining explicit consent from data subjects, and providing transparency about data usage.

Data security is another critical concern, as data breaches can have severe consequences for organizations and individuals. Implementing encryption, access controls, and regular security audits helps protect sensitive data from unauthorized access and breaches. Organizations must also stay informed about emerging threats and continuously update their security practices to mitigate risks.

In conclusion, understanding data sources and acquisition methods is fundamental for harnessing the power of data in business. Internal data sources, such as transactional records, CRM systems, and ERP systems, provide a solid foundation for analysis. External data sources, including market research reports, social media platforms, government databases, and third-party providers, offer valuable additional insights. Employing various data acquisition methods, from web scraping and APIs to IoT devices and surveys, ensures that organizations collect comprehensive and accurate data. Addressing challenges related to data quality, privacy, and security is essential for maintaining trust and compliance. By mastering data sources and acquisition methods, businesses can unlock the full potential of their data and drive informed, strategic decisions.

Mastering data sources and acquisition methods also involves continuously evaluating and updating these processes to adapt to new technologies and changing business environments. As the data landscape evolves, organizations must remain agile and open to integrating new data sources and acquisition techniques. This proactive approach ensures that data remains relevant, timely, and actionable, supporting ongoing innovation and growth.

Data Quality and Integrity

Ensuring data quality and integrity is crucial for any organization relying on data-driven decision-making. High-quality data supports accurate analysis, reliable insights, and informed strategies, while compromised data can lead to erroneous conclusions and costly mistakes. This chapter delves into the key aspects of data quality and integrity, offering practical advice on maintaining and improving these critical elements.

Data quality refers to the condition of data based on factors such as accuracy, completeness, consistency, timeliness, and relevance. Accurate data correctly represents the real-world entity it describes. For example, a customer's name or address must be correctly recorded to ensure accurate communication and service delivery. Completeness means that all required data is present; missing data can lead to incomplete analysis and misguided decisions. Consistency involves ensuring that data is uniform across different systems and databases, preventing discrepancies that can arise from duplication or data entry errors. Timeliness ensures that data is up-to-date and available when needed, which is particularly crucial in fast-paced environments like finance and logistics. Relevance ensures that the data collected is aligned with the organization's goals and needs.

Data integrity, meanwhile, focuses on maintaining and assuring the accuracy and consistency of data over its entire lifecycle. This includes protecting data from unauthorized access or alterations, ensuring it remains intact and uncorrupted. Integrity is about the trustworthiness of the data and involves processes like validation, audit trails, and access controls.

One of the first steps in ensuring data quality is implementing robust data governance practices. Data governance defines the policies, procedures, and responsibilities for data management across the organization. It establishes clear guidelines for data ownership, quality standards, and usage policies. A strong data governance framework involves collaboration between various stakeholders, including IT, legal, compliance, and business units, to ensure that data practices align with organizational objectives and regulatory requirements.

Data validation is another critical component of maintaining data quality. Validation checks ensure that data entered into systems meets predefined criteria, such as format, range, and consistency requirements. For instance, a simple validation rule might check that a date of birth field contains a valid date and that the age calculated from this date falls within a reasonable range. More complex validation might involve cross-referencing data against other databases to verify accuracy. Implementing validation at the point of data entry helps catch errors early, reducing the need for costly data cleaning later on.

Regular data cleaning and maintenance are essential tasks to address issues like duplicates, inaccuracies, and obsolete information. Data cleaning involves identifying and correcting errors, standardizing formats, and removing duplicates. For example, customer records might be cleaned to merge duplicate entries, correct spelling mistakes, and update outdated contact information. Regular maintenance involves periodic reviews to ensure data remains current and relevant. This might include purging outdated records, verifying data accuracy through audits, and updating information based on new inputs.

Data profiling is a technique used to assess the quality of data by examining its content, structure, and relationships. Profiling tools analyze datasets to identify patterns, anomalies, and potential issues. For example, profiling might reveal that a significant percentage of email addresses in a customer database are invalid, prompting an initiative to clean and update this data. Profiling helps organizations understand the state of their data and prioritize areas for improvement.

Metadata management plays a crucial role in ensuring data quality and integrity. Metadata is data about data, providing context and meaning to the underlying information. It includes details like data source, format, definitions, and usage rules. Effective metadata management ensures that data is well-documented, making it easier to understand, access, and use. For instance, a well-maintained metadata repository can help data analysts quickly find relevant datasets, understand their structure, and apply the appropriate analysis techniques.

Data lineage tracks the origin, movement, and transformation of data through various systems and processes. Understanding data lineage helps ensure data integrity by providing visibility into how data flows and changes over time. It allows organizations to trace errors back to their source, assess the impact of changes, and ensure that data transformations are accurately documented. For example, if an error is detected in a report, data lineage can help identify whether the issue originated from an incorrect data entry, a flawed transformation process, or an external data source.

Ensuring data quality and integrity also involves implementing robust security measures to protect data from unauthorized access, breaches, and corruption. Data encryption, both at rest and in transit, ensures that data remains secure from interception and unauthorized access. Access controls, such as role-based access and multi-factor authentication, limit data access to authorized personnel only. Regular security audits and vulnerability assessments help identify and mitigate potential risks, ensuring that data remains protected.

Data quality and integrity are also influenced by the human factor. Training and awareness programs are essential to educate employees about the importance of data quality and the role they play in maintaining it. This includes training on proper data entry techniques, understanding validation rules, and recognizing the impact of errors. Encouraging a culture of accountability and attention to detail can significantly improve data quality and integrity.

Automating data quality processes can enhance efficiency and reduce the likelihood of errors. Automation tools can handle repetitive tasks like data validation, cleaning, and profiling, freeing up human resources for more strategic activities. For example, automated scripts can regularly scan databases for duplicates, validate new entries against predefined rules, and generate reports on data quality metrics. Automation not only improves accuracy but also ensures that data quality processes are consistently applied across the organization.

Finally, continuous monitoring and improvement are key to maintaining high data quality and integrity. Establishing metrics and KPIs (Key Performance Indicators) for data quality helps track performance and identify areas for improvement. Regularly reviewing these metrics allows organizations to address issues promptly and adjust their strategies as needed. For example, if a KPI shows a rising number of data entry errors, the organization might investigate the root cause, provide additional training, or enhance validation rules.

In conclusion, maintaining data quality and integrity is a multifaceted endeavor that requires a combination of governance, validation, cleaning, profiling, metadata management, and security measures. By implementing robust data governance practices, validating data at the point of entry, regularly cleaning and maintaining datasets, and leveraging metadata and data lineage, organizations can ensure that their data remains accurate, complete, and reliable. Automation and continuous monitoring further enhance these efforts, providing a solid foundation for data-driven decision-making and strategic initiatives. Emphasizing the importance of data quality and fostering a culture of accountability and continuous improvement will empower organizations to unlock the full potential of their data, driving better outcomes and sustained success.

Addressing data quality and integrity is not just a technical challenge but also an organizational one. Cultivating a data-centric culture where every member understands and values the importance of data quality can make a significant difference. This involves leadership buy-in, clear communication of data quality goals, and the establishment of best practices across the organization.

Data Storage Solutions: Databases and Data Warehouses

Choosing the right data storage solution is critical for any organization that wants to efficiently manage, store, and retrieve vast amounts of data. Databases and data warehouses serve distinct purposes, and understanding their differences, strengths, and appropriate use cases can significantly impact the effectiveness of your data management strategy.

Databases are the workhorses of day-to-day operations, designed to handle a continuous stream of transactions. They are optimized for quick reads and writes, making them ideal for applications where data is constantly being updated, such as customer relationship management (CRM) systems, e-commerce platforms, and online transaction processing (OLTP) systems. Databases store data in structured formats using tables, rows, and columns, which allows for efficient querying and data manipulation using SQL (Structured Query Language).

One of the most common types of databases is the relational database management system (RDBMS), which includes well-known systems such as MySQL, PostgreSQL, Oracle, and Microsoft SQL Server. These systems enforce schema consistency and data integrity through constraints, indexes, and relationships between tables. For example, a retail business might use an RDBMS to manage inventory levels, track sales transactions, and maintain customer records, ensuring that each piece of information is accurately linked and easily accessible.

In contrast, NoSQL databases offer a more flexible approach to data storage by supporting a variety of data models, including document, key-value, column-family, and graph models. These databases are designed to handle unstructured or semi-structured data, making them suitable for applications like content management systems, real-time analytics, and large-scale distributed systems. MongoDB, Cassandra, and Redis are popular examples of NoSQL databases. They excel in scenarios where data structures can vary and evolve over time, such as social media platforms that need to store diverse types of user-generated content.

When an organization needs to analyze large volumes of historical data, often aggregated from various sources, a data warehouse becomes essential. Data warehouses are optimized for read-heavy operations and complex queries, making them ideal for business intelligence (BI) and analytics. Unlike operational databases that handle frequent updates, data warehouses are designed for batch processing and analytical workloads, which involve summarizing, aggregating, and analyzing data over time.

A data warehouse typically follows a star or snowflake schema, which organizes data into fact and dimension tables. Fact tables store quantitative data, such as sales figures, while dimension tables store descriptive attributes, such as time, geography, and product details. This structure allows for efficient querying and reporting, enabling analysts to generate insights from large datasets. For instance, a retail company might use a data warehouse to analyze sales trends across different regions and time periods, helping them make informed decisions about inventory management and marketing strategies.

One of the key components of a data warehouse is the ETL (Extract, Transform, Load) process. ETL involves extracting data from various sources, transforming it into a consistent format, and loading it into the data warehouse. This process ensures that the data is clean, accurate, and ready for analysis. For example, a financial institution might extract transaction data from multiple systems, transform it to ensure consistency in currency formats and account identifiers, and load it into a data warehouse for comprehensive financial reporting.

Cloud-based data warehousing solutions, such as Amazon Redshift, Google BigQuery, and Snowflake, have gained popularity due to their scalability, flexibility, and ease of use. These platforms offer the ability to scale storage and compute resources independently, allowing organizations to handle varying workloads without significant upfront investment in hardware. Additionally, cloud-based solutions often include built-in features for data security, backup, and disaster recovery, reducing the administrative burden on IT teams.

Choosing between a database and a data warehouse depends on the specific needs of your organization. If your primary goal is to manage day-to-day transactions and ensure data consistency, a database is the right choice. On the other hand, if you need to perform complex analyses and generate insights from large volumes of historical data, a data warehouse is more suitable.

In some cases, organizations might benefit from using both databases and data warehouses in a complementary manner. For example, an e-commerce company could use a database to manage real-time inventory and order processing, while simultaneously using a data warehouse to analyze customer purchasing patterns and optimize marketing campaigns. This hybrid approach leverages the strengths of both systems, ensuring efficient transaction processing and robust data analysis capabilities.

Another important consideration is the integration of data from diverse sources. Modern organizations often rely on a variety of data systems, including databases, data warehouses, and third-party applications. Ensuring seamless data integration is crucial for maintaining data quality and enabling comprehensive analysis. Tools such as data integration platforms and middleware can facilitate the flow of data between systems, ensuring that all relevant information is available for decision-making.

Data governance and security are also critical aspects of any data storage solution. Databases and data warehouses must comply with regulatory requirements and protect sensitive information from unauthorized access. Implementing robust access controls, encryption, and audit logging can help safeguard data and ensure compliance with standards such as GDPR (General Data Protection Regulation) and HIPAA (Health Insurance Portability and Accountability Act). For example, a healthcare provider must ensure that patient data stored in databases and data warehouses is encrypted and accessible only to authorized personnel.

Performance optimization is another key factor to consider. Databases and data warehouses must be tuned to handle the specific workloads they are designed for. This might involve indexing, partitioning, and optimizing query performance. For instance, an RDBMS might use indexes to speed up search queries, while a data warehouse might use partitioning to distribute data across multiple storage devices, enhancing query performance for large datasets.

Emerging technologies such as in-memory databases and data lakes are also worth exploring. In-memory databases, like SAP HANA, store data in RAM rather than on disk, enabling ultra-fast read and write operations. They are particularly useful for applications requiring real-time analytics and rapid transaction processing. Data lakes, on the other hand, provide a scalable and flexible storage solution for large volumes of raw data in its native format. They are ideal for organizations that need to store and analyze diverse data types, including structured, semi-structured, and unstructured data.

In conclusion, selecting the right data storage solution involves understanding the specific needs of your organization and the strengths of various technologies. Databases are essential for managing real-time transactions and ensuring data consistency, while data warehouses are optimized for complex analyses and business intelligence. By leveraging both types of systems, integrating data from multiple sources, and implementing robust governance and security measures, organizations can effectively manage their data and derive valuable insights to drive strategic decision-making. As technology evolves, staying informed about emerging trends and continuously optimizing your data storage solutions will ensure that your organization remains agile and competitive in a data-driven world.

The evolution of data storage solutions doesn't stop with databases and data warehouses. As organizations strive to become more data-driven, they must also consider the role of data lakes and hybrid architectures in their overall data strategy.

Data Privacy and Ethical Considerations

Data privacy and ethical considerations are paramount in today's digital age, where data breaches and misuse can have severe consequences for individuals and organizations alike. Understanding and implementing robust data privacy measures and adhering to ethical standards is not just a regulatory requirement but a fundamental responsibility for anyone handling data.

Data privacy revolves around protecting personal information from unauthorized access, use, or disclosure. It involves implementing policies and practices that ensure data is collected, stored, and processed securely and transparently. One of the key frameworks guiding data privacy in many parts of the world is the General Data Protection Regulation

(GDPR). The GDPR sets stringent requirements for how personal data must be handled and gives individuals significant control over their own data.

Consider a scenario where a company collects customer data through its website. Under GDPR, the company must obtain explicit consent from users before collecting their data. This means clear, affirmative action must be taken by the user—pre-ticked checkboxes or implied consent are not sufficient. The company must also inform users about how their data will be used, who it will be shared with, and how long it will be retained. This transparency is crucial in building trust and ensuring compliance with data protection laws.

Another vital aspect of data privacy is ensuring data security. Organizations must implement technical and organizational measures to protect data from breaches. This includes encryption, access controls, and regular security audits. For instance, encrypting sensitive data ensures that even if it is intercepted during transmission, it cannot be read by unauthorized parties. Similarly, access controls restrict data access to only those employees who need it to perform their job functions, thereby reducing the risk of internal data misuse.

Beyond compliance, ethical considerations in data handling are equally important. Ethical data practices involve respecting the rights and freedoms of individuals and ensuring that data usage aligns with societal values. One of the core principles of ethical data usage is the concept of data minimization. This principle dictates that organizations should only collect and retain the minimum amount of data necessary to achieve their objectives. For example, if a mobile app requires access to a user's location data to provide localized weather updates, it should not also collect data unrelated to its primary function, such as the user's contact list.

Ethical considerations also extend to how data is analyzed and used. With the rise of big data and advanced analytics, organizations can gain deep insights from data, but this power must be wielded responsibly. For instance, predictive analytics can help businesses anticipate customer needs and tailor their offerings accordingly. However, these techniques must not infringe on individual privacy or lead to discriminatory practices. For example, using data to predict creditworthiness should be done in a way that avoids bias and ensures fairness.

One notable case that highlights the importance of ethical data use is the Cambridge Analytica scandal. The company harvested data from millions of Facebook users without their consent and used it for targeted political advertising. This breach of trust underscored the need for stringent data privacy measures and sparked global discussions about the ethical use of data. Organizations must learn from such incidents and prioritize ethical considerations in their data practices to avoid similar pitfalls.

Transparency is another cornerstone of ethical data practices. Organizations must be open about their data collection, usage, and sharing practices. This involves clear communication with users about how their data will be used and obtaining informed consent. Transparency also means being honest about data breaches. If a breach occurs, affected individuals should be notified promptly so they can take steps to protect themselves. For example, if a company's customer database is compromised, it should inform customers about the breach, the steps being taken to address it, and how customers can protect their accounts.

In addition to transparency and consent, data privacy and ethics also encompass the right to be forgotten. This principle allows individuals to request the deletion of their personal data when it is no longer needed for its original purpose. For example, if a customer closes their account with an online retailer, they should have the right to request the deletion of their personal data from the retailer's database. Implementing this right requires organizations to have processes in place for responding to such requests and ensuring that data is permanently deleted from all systems.

Employee training and awareness are critical components of data privacy and ethical practices. Employees must understand the importance of data protection and be aware of the policies and procedures in place. Regular training sessions can help reinforce the importance of data privacy and keep employees updated on the latest regulations and best practices. For example, employees should be trained on how to recognize phishing attempts and the importance of using strong, unique passwords for accessing sensitive data.

Data privacy and ethics also intersect with the concept of data sovereignty, which refers to the idea that data is subject to the laws and regulations of the country in which it is collected. This is particularly relevant for organizations that operate internationally and must navigate a complex landscape of data protection laws. For example, an organization based in the United States that collects data from European customers must comply with GDPR, even though its primary operations are in a different jurisdiction. Understanding and adhering to these regulations is essential for maintaining compliance and avoiding legal repercussions.

Finally, fostering a culture of data ethics within an organization requires leadership commitment. Executives and managers must lead by example, demonstrating a commitment to data privacy and ethical practices. This involves not only setting policies and procedures but also creating an environment where ethical considerations are valued and prioritized. For instance, leaders can promote ethical decision-making by encouraging employees to speak up if they have concerns about data practices and by ensuring that these concerns are addressed promptly and transparently.

In conclusion, data privacy and ethical considerations are not just legal obligations but fundamental responsibilities for any organization handling data. By implementing robust data protection measures, respecting individual rights, and fostering a culture of transparency and ethics, organizations can build trust with their customers and stakeholders. This trust is essential for sustainable growth and success in the digital age. As technology continues to evolve, staying informed about emerging privacy issues and adapting practices accordingly will be key to navigating the complexities of data privacy and ethics.

Data privacy and ethical considerations also play a critical role in the design and implementation of new technologies and services. Integrating privacy by design and privacy by default principles into the development process ensures that data protection is central to the system's architecture. Privacy by design means that privacy measures are integrated into the technology from the outset, rather than being an afterthought. Privacy by default ensures that the default settings of a system or service provide the highest level of privacy protection.

Chapter 3

Data Preparation and Cleaning

The Importance of Data Preparation

Data preparation is the cornerstone of any successful data analysis or machine learning project. It involves transforming raw data into a clean and organized format, ready for analysis. This process might not seem as glamorous as building predictive models or visualizing data insights, but it is crucial. Proper data preparation can significantly impact the accuracy and reliability of your results, making it an essential skill for anyone working with data.

Imagine you are a chef preparing a gourmet meal. Before you even start cooking, you need to ensure that all your ingredients are fresh, measured correctly, and ready to use. Similarly, data preparation involves cleaning and organizing your data so that it is ready for analysis. This process typically includes steps such as data cleaning, data transformation, and data integration.

Data cleaning is often the first and most critical step in data preparation. It involves identifying and correcting errors, such as missing values, duplicates, and outliers. For instance, consider a dataset containing customer information for a retail business. If some entries have missing values for key fields like age or location, it can skew your analysis. Techniques such as imputation, where missing values are filled in based on other available data, can help address this issue. Alternatively, you might choose to remove rows with missing values if they are not critical to your analysis.

Duplicate entries can also pose significant challenges. For example, if you are analyzing sales data and the same transaction is recorded multiple times, it can inflate your sales figures and lead to incorrect conclusions. Identifying and removing duplicates is essential to ensure the accuracy of your analysis. Similarly, outliers—data points that are significantly different from others—can distort your results. For example, a single transaction of $1,000,000 in a dataset where most transactions are below $100 can skew your analysis. Outliers should be carefully examined to determine whether they represent errors or genuine variations.

Once the data is clean, the next step is data transformation. This involves converting data into a format suitable for analysis. For instance, you might need to normalize numerical data to ensure that all variables are on the same scale. Imagine you are analyzing the performance of various stores based on their sales and customer footfall. If sales are measured in thousands and footfall in hundreds, the disparity in scales can affect your analysis. Normalizing the data ensures that each variable contributes equally to the analysis.

Data transformation can also involve encoding categorical variables. Many machine learning algorithms require numerical input, so categorical data needs to be converted into numerical form. For example, if you have a dataset with a "Color" column containing values like "Red," "Green," and "Blue," you can use techniques like one-hot encoding to convert these into numerical values. This might result in three new columns, each representing one of the colors, with binary values indicating the presence or absence of that color.

Data integration is another crucial aspect of data preparation. This involves combining data from different sources to create a unified dataset. For example, a business might have customer data stored in a CRM system, sales data in an ERP system, and web traffic data in a web analytics tool. Integrating these datasets can provide a comprehensive view of customer behavior and help identify patterns and trends. However, data integration can be challenging due to differences in data formats, structures, and quality across sources. Ensuring consistency and accuracy during integration is vital for reliable analysis.

Consider a scenario where a company wants to analyze customer behavior to improve its marketing strategy. The company has data from multiple sources: purchase history from the sales department, customer demographics from the marketing department, and website interaction data from the IT department. Integrating these datasets can provide a holistic view of customer behavior, enabling more targeted and effective marketing strategies. However, differences in data formats—such as varying name formats (e.g., "John Doe" vs. "Doe, John") and inconsistencies in address fields—can complicate the integration process. Standardizing data formats and resolving discrepancies is crucial for successful data integration.

Another important aspect of data preparation is feature engineering. This involves creating new features from existing data to improve the performance of machine learning models. For example, if you are working with a dataset containing dates, you might create new features such as the day of the week, month, or year to capture temporal patterns in the data. Similarly, for a dataset containing text data, you might extract features such as word counts, sentiment scores, or keyword presence to enhance the predictive power of your models.

Feature selection is also a critical part of data preparation. This involves identifying the most relevant features for your analysis or model. Including too many features can lead to overfitting, where the model performs well on the training data but poorly on new, unseen data. Feature selection techniques, such as recursive feature elimination or principal component analysis, can help identify the most important features and reduce dimensionality, improving model performance and interpretability.

Data preparation also involves ensuring data quality and consistency. This includes verifying data accuracy, completeness, and reliability. For example, if you are analyzing customer feedback data, you need to ensure that the feedback is accurately captured and consistently formatted. Inconsistent data can lead to misleading insights and incorrect conclusions. Establishing data quality checks and validation processes can help maintain data integrity and ensure reliable analysis.

Automation can play a significant role in data preparation. Manual data cleaning and transformation can be time-consuming and error-prone, especially for large datasets. Automation tools and scripts can streamline the process, reducing the likelihood of errors and improving efficiency. For example, data cleaning scripts can automatically identify and correct common issues such as missing values, duplicates, and outliers. Similarly, data transformation pipelines can automate the process of normalizing data, encoding categorical variables, and generating new features, ensuring consistency and reproducibility.

Documentation is another essential aspect of data preparation. Keeping detailed records of the data preparation process, including the steps taken, techniques used, and decisions made, is crucial for transparency and reproducibility. Documentation helps ensure that the data preparation process can be reviewed, understood, and replicated by others, facilitating collaboration and improving the reliability of your analysis.

In conclusion, data preparation is a vital step in any data analysis or machine learning project. It involves cleaning, transforming, and integrating data to ensure accuracy, consistency, and suitability for analysis. Proper data preparation can significantly impact the quality and reliability of your results, making it an essential skill for anyone working with data. By understanding and implementing effective data preparation techniques, you can unlock the full potential of your data and drive meaningful insights and outcomes.

Additionally, data preparation is not a one-time effort but an ongoing process. As new data is collected, it must be consistently cleaned, transformed, and integrated to maintain the quality and relevance of your dataset. This continuous cycle ensures that your analysis remains accurate and up-to-date, reflecting the most current information available.

Techniques for Data Cleaning

Data cleaning is a critical process in data analysis and one that significantly influences the quality and reliability of results. It involves identifying and rectifying errors and inconsistencies in data to ensure it is accurate, complete, and ready for analysis. Without proper data cleaning, even the most sophisticated analytical tools or models can produce misleading or erroneous insights. The following techniques for data cleaning provide a comprehensive approach to preparing data for analysis.

The first step in data cleaning is identifying and handling missing values. Missing data can occur due to various reasons, such as data entry errors, system failures, or incomplete data collection processes. There are several strategies to address missing values, each depending on the nature of the data and the extent of the missing information. One common method is deletion, which involves removing rows or columns with missing values. This approach is only suitable when the amount of missing data is minimal and doesn't significantly impact the dataset. However, in cases where deletion would result in substantial data loss, imputation techniques are employed. Imputation involves replacing missing values with substituted ones, such as the mean, median, or mode of the respective column. More sophisticated imputation methods use algorithms to predict missing values based on other available data.

Next, the detection and removal of duplicate records are essential to ensure data integrity. Duplicates can arise from multiple data entry points, system integrations, or even errors in data collection processes. For instance, in a customer database, if the same customer is recorded multiple times, it can lead to overestimation in metrics like customer count or total sales. Identifying duplicates involves checking for identical rows or records with slight variations, such as different cases in names or minor typographical errors. Once identified, these duplicates can be merged or removed, ensuring that each unique entity is represented only once in the dataset.

Outliers are another critical aspect of data cleaning. Outliers are data points that deviate significantly from the rest of the dataset. They can result from measurement errors, data entry mistakes, or genuine but rare events. For example, in a sales dataset, a single transaction worth millions in a dataset where most transactions are in the range of hundreds or thousands can significantly affect the analysis. Outlier detection techniques include statistical methods such as the Z-score, which measures how many standard deviations a data point is from the mean, and the IQR (Interquartile Range) method, which identifies data points that lie beyond the typical range. Once detected, outliers can be handled by either removing them, if they are errors, or treating them separately if they represent valid but extreme cases.

Standardization and normalization of data are also crucial steps in data cleaning, particularly for numerical data. Standardization involves rescaling data to have a mean of zero and a standard deviation of one. This process is essential when data features have different units and scales, which can skew the analysis. For instance, in a dataset containing both income (in dollars) and age (in years), the differences in scale can affect the weight each variable has in the analysis. Normalization, on the other hand, rescales data to a range of [0, 1] or [-1, 1], ensuring that no single feature dominates due to its scale. These processes help in making the data homogeneous, enhancing the performance of many machine learning algorithms that are sensitive to the scale of input data.

Data type conversion is another critical aspect of data cleaning. Often, data collected from various sources may come in formats that are not suitable for analysis. For example, numerical data might be stored as text, or dates might be in inconsistent formats. Converting these data types to appropriate formats ensures that mathematical operations and comparisons can be accurately performed. For instance, converting date strings to date objects allows for easier computation of time intervals and the identification of temporal patterns.

Handling inconsistent data is another important technique in data cleaning. Inconsistencies can occur in various forms, such as differing formats for the same variable (e.g., "NY" vs. "New York") or different units of measurement (e.g., inches vs. centimeters). Standardizing these inconsistencies is crucial for accurate analysis. Techniques include creating mapping tables that convert different representations of the same value into a consistent format or using regular expressions to identify and correct formatting issues.

Addressing data entry errors is also vital. These errors can include typographical mistakes, incorrect values, or misplaced decimal points. Automated tools can help identify and correct common data entry errors, but manual inspection is often necessary for more complex issues. For example, if a dataset contains a column for age and an entry reads "250," it is likely an error that needs correction, as it falls outside the plausible range for human age.

Another technique for data cleaning is handling categorical data, especially when dealing with text. Categorical data often needs to be encoded into numerical values for analysis. Techniques such as one-hot encoding can convert categorical variables into binary vectors, making them suitable for machine learning algorithms. For example, a "Color" column with values "Red," "Green," and "Blue" can be transformed into three binary columns, each representing one of the colors. This process ensures that categorical data is properly utilized in the analysis without introducing bias.

Consistency checks are also an integral part of data cleaning. These checks ensure that data follows specific rules or constraints. For example, in a dataset of employees, the "Hire Date" should always precede the "Termination Date." Automated scripts can be developed to perform these checks and flag any inconsistencies for further investigation. Ensuring consistency helps in maintaining the reliability and accuracy of the dataset.

Data enrichment is another useful technique in data cleaning. This involves augmenting the dataset with additional information from external sources to fill in gaps or provide more context. For example, adding demographic information based on postal codes or appending weather data to sales records can provide deeper insights. However, it is crucial to ensure that the added data is accurate and relevant to the analysis.

Regular audits and validation are essential to maintaining data quality over time. Data cleaning should not be a one-time task but an ongoing process. Regular audits involve periodically reviewing the dataset to identify and correct any emerging issues. Validation techniques, such as cross-validation, can help ensure that the data cleaning process has not introduced any biases or errors. Implementing automated data quality monitoring tools can provide real-time alerts for any anomalies, enabling prompt corrective actions.

Documentation is a final but critical part of the data cleaning process. Keeping detailed records of the steps taken, decisions made, and techniques used ensures transparency and reproducibility. This documentation is invaluable for future reference and for other team members who may work with the data. It also helps in maintaining consistency in data cleaning practices across different projects and datasets.

In conclusion, data cleaning is an essential process that underpins the accuracy and reliability of data analysis. By employing techniques such as handling missing values, removing duplicates, detecting outliers, standardizing data, converting data types, addressing inconsistencies, correcting data entry errors, encoding categorical data, performing consistency checks, enriching data, and conducting regular audits and documentation, one can ensure that the data is of high quality and ready for meaningful analysis. Mastering these techniques not only enhances the quality of insights derived from the data but also builds a solid foundation for any data-driven decision-making process.

Effective data cleaning is not just about applying technical techniques; it also involves understanding the context of the data and the specific requirements of the analysis. This understanding enables data scientists and analysts to make informed decisions about which cleaning methods are most appropriate and how to apply them in a way that preserves the integrity of the data.

Handling Missing Data

Handling missing data is one of the most critical aspects of data analysis. It involves dealing with gaps in datasets where values are not recorded or are missing for various reasons. These gaps can significantly impact the results of any analysis or model, making it essential to address them effectively. The approach to handling missing data can vary depending on the nature of the data, the extent of the missing values, and the intended analysis. This chapter delves into practical techniques for identifying, understanding, and addressing missing data to ensure robust analysis and reliable results.

Missing data can occur at any stage of data collection and for numerous reasons. It might be due to human error during data entry, equipment malfunction, non-response in surveys, or even deliberate omission. Understanding why data is missing is the first step in handling it. There are three main types of missing data: Missing Completely at Random (MCAR), Missing at Random (MAR), and Missing Not at Random (MNAR). MCAR occurs when the likelihood of missing data on a variable is independent of any other observed or unobserved data. MAR happens when the missingness is related to some observed data but not the missing data itself. MNAR occurs when the missingness is related to the value of the missing data itself and is often the most challenging to handle.

The identification of missing data is straightforward in most cases. Many datasets will have specific indicators for missing values, such as NaN (Not a

Number), blanks, or specific codes like -999. Tools like pandas in Python or dplyr in R offer functions to detect missing values. Once identified, it's crucial to quantify the extent of the missing data. Summarizing the missing data through visualizations, such as heat maps or bar charts, can provide a clear picture of the distribution and patterns of missingness across the dataset.

One common technique for handling missing data is deletion, which involves removing rows or columns with missing values. This method is simple and effective when the proportion of missing data is small. However, deletion can lead to significant data loss and potential bias if the missing data is not MCAR. For example, in a medical study, if patients with missing data are systematically different from those without missing data, deleting them could skew the results.

Imputation is another widely used technique where missing values are replaced with substituted values. Simple imputation methods include filling in missing data with the mean, median, or mode of the respective column. This approach is easy to implement but can underestimate the variance and distort relationships between variables. A more sophisticated method is regression imputation, where a regression model predicts the missing values based on other available data. For instance, in a dataset of house prices, missing values for square footage might be predicted using other features like the number of bedrooms and the location.

Another advanced imputation method is multiple imputation, which involves creating multiple datasets with different imputed values and then averaging the results. This technique accounts for the uncertainty around the missing data and provides more robust estimates. Multiple imputation can be particularly useful in large datasets with complex interdependencies between variables.

K-Nearest Neighbors (KNN) imputation is another technique that can be effective, especially when the data has a strong local structure. KNN imputation replaces missing values with the average of the nearest neighbors' values. For example, in a dataset of customer purchases, missing values for the amount spent might be imputed based on the average amount spent by the nearest customers in terms of demographics and purchasing behavior.

In cases where the missing data is MNAR, traditional imputation methods might not be sufficient. One approach to handle MNAR data is to model the missingness explicitly. This can involve using more complex statistical models or machine learning algorithms that incorporate the process of missingness into the analysis. For example, in longitudinal studies where dropout rates might be related to the outcome of interest, joint modeling of the outcome and the dropout process can provide more accurate estimates.

Sensitivity analysis is another important aspect of handling missing data. It involves assessing how the results of the analysis change under different assumptions about the missing data. By performing sensitivity analysis, analysts can understand the potential impact of the missing data on their conclusions and make more informed decisions. For instance, in a survey where some respondents did not answer certain questions, sensitivity analysis can help determine whether the missing responses significantly affect the survey's overall findings.

Documentation and transparency are crucial when handling missing data. Analysts should document the extent of the missing data, the methods used to handle it, and any assumptions made during the process. This documentation ensures that the analysis is reproducible and that other stakeholders can understand and evaluate the handling of missing data. For example, if a dataset undergoes multiple imputation, the imputation process, including the models used and the number of imputations, should be clearly documented.

Using domain knowledge can also improve the handling of missing data. Understanding the context and the potential reasons for missingness can guide the choice of imputation methods and ensure that the imputed values are plausible. For instance, in a dataset of agricultural yields, domain knowledge might suggest that missing values for crop yield in a particular region during a specific year could be due to known events like droughts or pest outbreaks. This information can be used to inform the imputation process and improve the accuracy of the results.

Finally, it's important to consider the implications of missing data on the overall analysis and decision-making process. Even with sophisticated imputation methods, the presence of missing data introduces uncertainty that should be acknowledged and communicated. Analysts should be cautious in interpreting results and making decisions based on datasets with significant missing data. For example, in policy-making, decisions based on incomplete data should be made with an understanding of the limitations and potential biases introduced by the missing data.

Handling missing data is a complex but essential task in data analysis. By understanding the nature of the missing data, employing appropriate techniques for imputation or deletion, and carefully documenting the process, analysts can mitigate the impact of missing data and ensure more reliable and accurate results. The strategies discussed in this chapter provide a comprehensive approach to addressing missing data, enabling robust analysis and informed decision-making.

Incorporating robust strategies for handling missing data is crucial for ensuring the integrity of statistical analyses and machine learning models. Beyond the techniques already discussed, there are additional nuanced approaches and considerations that can further refine how missing data is managed in different contexts.

Data Transformation and Normalization

Data transformation and normalization are fundamental processes in data analysis, crucial for preparing raw data for modeling and analysis. Without these steps, data can be inconsistent, noisy, and difficult to interpret, leading to unreliable results. This chapter delves into the techniques and principles of data transformation and normalization, providing practical advice for beginners to tackle these essential tasks effectively.

Data transformation involves converting data from its raw format into a more suitable structure for analysis. This process can include changing data types, aggregating data, or creating new variables. One common transformation is converting categorical data into numerical form. For instance, when dealing with survey responses like "Yes," "No," and "Maybe," these categories can be encoded as 1, 0, and 2, respectively. This conversion allows for numerical analysis and modeling techniques that require numerical inputs.

Another transformation technique is the use of logarithms to handle skewed data. In many datasets, certain variables may exhibit a skewed distribution, where a few large values dominate. Applying a logarithmic transformation can compress these values, reducing skewness and making the data more normally distributed. For example, income data often benefits from a log transformation, as it typically has a long tail of very high values.

Normalization, on the other hand, adjusts the scale of data to ensure consistency across different variables. This process is essential when variables have different units or scales. For example, in a dataset containing both age (measured in years) and income (measured in dollars), normalization ensures that neither variable disproportionately influences the analysis due to its larger scale. One common normalization technique is min-max scaling, which rescales the data to a fixed range, usually 0 to 1. This method involves subtracting the minimum value of the variable and then dividing by the range (the difference between the maximum and minimum values).

Another widely used normalization technique is z-score normalization, which transforms the data based on its mean and standard deviation. This method involves subtracting the mean of the variable and then dividing by the standard deviation, resulting in data with a mean of 0 and a standard deviation of 1. Z-score normalization is particularly useful when the data follows a normal distribution, as it standardizes the data into a common scale without distorting differences in the range of values.

When transforming and normalizing data, it is crucial to consider the context and the goals of the analysis. For instance, when dealing with time series data, transformations should preserve the temporal sequence of observations. Techniques such as differencing, which involves subtracting the previous observation from the current one, can help stabilize the mean of a time series and remove trends. This approach is often used in financial data analysis to make the data stationary, a requirement for many time series forecasting models.

In some cases, domain-specific knowledge can guide the choice of transformation and normalization techniques. For example, in image processing, pixel values are often normalized to a range of 0 to 1 to facilitate neural network training. Similarly, in genomics, read counts from sequencing data are transformed using techniques like the logarithm or the variance stabilizing transformation to handle the wide range of expression levels across genes.

Practical considerations also play a significant role in data transformation and normalization. When dealing with large datasets, computational efficiency becomes important. Vectorized operations, available in many programming languages and libraries, allow for efficient transformations without the need for explicit loops. For example, in Python, libraries like NumPy and pandas provide functions to perform transformations on entire arrays or data frames in a single operation, significantly speeding up the process.

Handling missing values is another critical aspect of data transformation. Before normalizing data, it is essential to address any missing values, as they can distort the results. Techniques for handling missing data include imputation, where missing values are replaced with estimated ones, and deletion, where rows or columns with missing values are removed. The choice of technique depends on the extent and pattern of missingness in the data. For example, if only a small proportion of data is missing and the missingness is random, deletion might be appropriate. However, if a significant portion of data is missing or the missingness is systematic, imputation methods like mean imputation, regression imputation, or multiple imputation may be more suitable.

Data transformation and normalization also play a crucial role in feature engineering, the process of creating new features from raw data to improve model performance. For example, polynomial transformations can create new features by raising existing features to a power, capturing non-linear relationships in the data. Interaction terms, which are products of two or more features, can also be created to capture interactions between variables. These transformations can significantly enhance the predictive power of models, especially in complex datasets with non-linear relationships.

In addition to improving model performance, data transformation and normalization can aid in data visualization. Many visualization techniques assume that data is on a common scale or normally distributed. Transforming and normalizing data can make patterns and relationships in the data more apparent, facilitating the identification of trends, outliers, and clusters. For instance, log-transforming a skewed variable can reveal underlying patterns that are not visible in the raw data.

While transforming and normalizing data, it is essential to maintain the interpretability of the data. Transformations should be reversible, allowing for the back-transformation of results to the original scale for interpretation and communication. For example, if a logarithmic transformation is applied to income data, the results of any analysis or model should be back-transformed using the exponential function to provide interpretable insights in terms of actual income values.

Documentation and reproducibility are also critical when performing data transformations and normalization. Detailed documentation of the transformations applied, including the rationale and the specific methods used, ensures that the analysis can be reproduced and validated by others. This practice is especially important in collaborative projects and in fields where regulatory compliance and transparency are required.

Finally, it is essential to evaluate the impact of data transformations and normalization on the analysis results. This evaluation can be done through exploratory data analysis (EDA) and model validation techniques. EDA involves visualizing the transformed data to assess its distribution and identify any remaining issues. Model validation techniques, such as cross-validation, can be used to compare the performance of models trained on transformed and normalized data against those trained on raw data, ensuring that the transformations improve model performance without introducing bias or overfitting.

Data transformation and normalization are indispensable steps in the data preprocessing pipeline. By converting raw data into a suitable format and scale, these processes enable more accurate and reliable analysis, enhance model performance, and facilitate data visualization and interpretation. Through careful application of transformation and normalization techniques, data analysts can unlock the full potential of their datasets, leading to more robust insights and better decision-making.

In the realm of data analysis, understanding the nuances of data transformation and normalization is akin to mastering the foundation of a complex structure. These processes ensure that the data fed into analytical models is both meaningful and manageable, providing a solid base for any subsequent analysis or predictive modeling. Beyond the technical aspects, they also contribute to the overall robustness and credibility of the findings, which is paramount in data-driven decision-making.

Tools for Data Preparation

Effective data preparation is a cornerstone of successful data analysis, and selecting the right tools for this task is essential. Data preparation involves cleaning, transforming, and enriching data to make it ready for analysis. This chapter discusses various tools that facilitate these processes, providing practical insights on their features, benefits, and how to use them effectively.

One of the most widely used tools for data preparation is Python, a versatile programming language known for its robust data manipulation libraries. Two of the most popular libraries in Python for data preparation are pandas and NumPy. Pandas provide data structures and functions needed to work seamlessly with structured data. With pandas, you can easily handle missing values, filter and sort data, and perform aggregations. NumPy, on the other hand, is excellent for numerical operations and working with arrays. Together, these libraries allow you to perform complex data manipulations with minimal code.

For those preferring a user-friendly interface over coding, Microsoft Excel remains a powerful tool for data preparation. Excel's functionalities extend beyond simple spreadsheets; it offers advanced features like pivot tables, data validation, and conditional formatting. These features are particularly useful for quickly summarizing data and identifying trends or outliers. Excel's ability to handle large datasets has improved significantly, making it a viable option for many data preparation tasks.

Another powerful tool in the data preparation arsenal is SQL, a language designed for managing and querying relational databases. SQL is indispensable for working with large datasets stored in databases. It allows you to filter, join, and aggregate data efficiently. SQL's power lies in its ability to perform complex queries that can extract meaningful insights from vast amounts of data. Learning SQL can be particularly beneficial if you frequently work with database systems like MySQL, PostgreSQL, or SQL Server.

For more automated data preparation, tools like Alteryx provide a comprehensive platform that combines data blending, preparation, and analytics. Alteryx is designed to streamline the data preparation process through its intuitive drag-and-drop interface, which allows users to build workflows without writing code. It supports data from a wide range of sources, including databases, cloud services, and spreadsheets. Alteryx's built-in tools for cleaning, transforming, and enriching data make it a powerful ally in preparing data for analysis.

Data analysts and scientists who deal with big data often turn to Apache Spark, a unified analytics engine for large-scale data processing. Spark's capabilities for distributed data processing make it ideal for handling massive datasets that do not fit into memory on a single machine. Spark provides high-level APIs in Java, Scala, Python, and R, making it accessible to a broad range of users. Its DataFrame and SQL modules allow for sophisticated data manipulation and querying, while its machine learning library, MLlib, provides tools for data preparation and feature engineering.

For those working in the R ecosystem, the tidyverse suite of packages is indispensable for data preparation. The tidyverse includes packages like dplyr for data manipulation, tidyr for data tidying, and readr for reading data into R. These packages are designed to work seamlessly together, making the process of cleaning and transforming data straightforward and efficient. The tidyverse's consistent syntax and powerful functions enable users to perform complex data manipulations with concise, readable code.

Data visualization tools also play a crucial role in data preparation by helping to identify patterns, trends, and anomalies in the data. Tools like Tableau and Power BI offer robust data visualization capabilities combined with data preparation features. Tableau Prep, for instance, allows users to clean and shape their data visually, providing a clear understanding of the data's structure and quality before analysis. Power BI's Power Query feature offers similar capabilities, enabling users to perform data transformations and enrich their data within the same environment they use for creating visualizations.

In the realm of cloud-based data preparation, Google DataPrep by Trifacta stands out. Google DataPrep provides an intelligent data preparation service that leverages machine learning to suggest transformations and cleaning steps based on the data's characteristics. Its intuitive interface allows users to interact with their data visually and apply transformations with just a few clicks. Google DataPrep integrates seamlessly with other Google Cloud services, making it an excellent choice for those already invested in the Google Cloud ecosystem.

Apache NiFi is another powerful tool for data preparation, particularly suited for automating data workflows. NiFi's user-friendly interface allows users to design data flows visually, with a wide array of processors for data ingestion, transformation, and delivery. Its ability to handle real-time data streams makes it ideal for applications requiring continuous data preparation, such as IoT data processing or log file analysis.

For teams looking to collaborate on data preparation tasks, tools like Dataiku and Talend provide robust platforms that support collaborative workflows. Dataiku offers a comprehensive suite for data preparation, exploration, and machine learning, with features that facilitate teamwork and version control. Its visual interface allows users to build data workflows collaboratively, while its support for coding in Python, R, and SQL caters to more technical users. Talend, on the other hand, offers an open-source data integration platform with extensive connectors for various data sources and built-in tools for data quality and transformation. Talend's collaborative features and enterprise-level capabilities make it a popular choice for organizations with complex data preparation needs.

When working with unstructured data, tools like Apache Hadoop and Elasticsearch provide powerful solutions for data preparation. Hadoop's ecosystem, including tools like Hive and Pig, allows users to process and transform large volumes of unstructured data efficiently. Elasticsearch, combined with its data ingestion tool Logstash and visualization tool Kibana (collectively known as the ELK stack), provides a robust platform for indexing, searching, and analyzing unstructured data. These tools are particularly effective for preparing data from logs, social media, and other unstructured sources for analysis.

In addition to these tools, many programming environments and integrated development environments (IDEs) offer features that facilitate data preparation. Jupyter Notebooks, for example, provide an interactive environment where users can combine code, visualizations, and narrative text in a single document. This interactivity makes Jupyter Notebooks ideal for exploring and preparing data, documenting the process, and sharing insights with others. Similarly, RStudio offers a comprehensive IDE for R, with features that support data preparation, visualization, and analysis in a cohesive environment.

Choosing the right tool for data preparation depends on various factors, including the nature of the data, the specific tasks involved, and the user's proficiency with the tool. While some tools excel in handling large-scale data or providing advanced automation, others are better suited for interactive exploration and visualization. Understanding the strengths and limitations of each tool is crucial for selecting the most appropriate one for your data preparation needs.

In conclusion, a wide array of tools is available to support the diverse tasks involved in data preparation. From programming languages like Python and R to visual interfaces like Alteryx and Tableau Prep, each tool offers unique features that cater to different aspects of data preparation. By leveraging these tools effectively, data analysts can ensure their data is clean, well-structured, and ready for insightful analysis, ultimately leading to more robust and reliable results.

Beyond the tools mentioned, it's also important to consider the evolving landscape of data preparation technologies. As data sources become more varied and complex, newer tools and platforms continually emerge to address specific challenges in data preparation.

Chapter 4

Exploratory Data Analysis (EDA)

Introduction to EDA

Exploratory Data Analysis (EDA) is a critical step in the data analysis process. It involves summarizing the main characteristics of a dataset, often using visual methods. EDA is not just about looking at the data; it's about understanding its underlying structure, detecting anomalies, testing hypotheses, and checking assumptions. This chapter delves into the principles and practices of EDA, providing practical advice for beginners to navigate this foundational aspect of data science.

Imagine you are handed a new dataset. It's akin to receiving a novel written in a foreign language. Before you can derive any meaningful insights, you need to familiarize yourself with the basic grammar and vocabulary. Similarly, EDA helps you understand the "language" of your data. It allows you to see patterns, spot outliers, and uncover relationships that are not immediately obvious.

The first step in EDA is to get an overview of the data. This typically involves loading the dataset and checking its structure. In Python, libraries such as pandas offer convenient functions like head(), info(), and describe() that provide a snapshot of the data. The head() function displays the first few rows of the dataset, giving you a quick look at the variables and their values. The info() function provides a concise summary of the DataFrame, including the number of non-null entries and the data type of each column. The describe() function generates descriptive statistics that summarize the central tendency, dispersion, and shape of the dataset's distribution.

Once you have a basic understanding of the dataset's structure, the next step is to clean the data. Data cleaning is an essential part of EDA, as real-world data is often messy. This can include handling missing values, correcting data types, and removing duplicate records. For instance, missing values can be dealt with by either removing the rows/columns with missing data or imputing them with appropriate values. The choice of method depends on the context and the nature of the data.

After cleaning the data, it's important to examine the distribution of each variable. This helps in understanding the spread and central tendency of the data. Visualizations such as histograms, box plots, and density plots are particularly useful for this purpose. A histogram shows the frequency distribution of a single variable, providing insights into its range and the presence of any skewness or kurtosis. Box plots, on the other hand, display the distribution of data based on a five-number summary: minimum, first quartile, median, third quartile, and maximum. They are excellent for detecting outliers. Density plots are smoothed versions of histograms and can help in comparing the distributions of multiple variables.

Understanding the relationships between variables is another key aspect of EDA. Scatter plots and pair plots are effective tools for this. Scatter plots illustrate the relationship between two continuous variables, revealing possible correlations or trends. Pair plots extend this concept by displaying scatter plots for all pairs of variables in a dataset, making it easier to spot relationships and interactions. Correlation matrices and heatmaps are also valuable for quantifying the strength and direction of relationships between variables. A correlation matrix shows the correlation coefficients between pairs of variables, while a heatmap visualizes this information using color gradients.

Categorical data requires a different approach. Bar plots and count plots are useful for visualizing the frequency distribution of categorical variables. A bar plot displays the count or frequency of each category, making it easy to see which categories are most common. Count plots are similar but are specifically designed for counting the occurrences of categorical variables.

Multivariate analysis is another powerful aspect of EDA. Techniques such as principal component analysis (PCA) and clustering can help in understanding the structure of high-dimensional data. PCA reduces the dimensionality of the data by transforming it into a set of linearly uncorrelated variables called principal components. This is particularly useful for visualizing high-dimensional data in two or three dimensions. Clustering, on the other hand, groups data points into clusters based on their similarities. Algorithms like k-means and hierarchical clustering can reveal natural groupings in the data, providing insights into its underlying structure.

While visualizations are a vital part of EDA, summary statistics also play a crucial role. Measures of central tendency (mean, median, mode) and measures of dispersion (range, variance, standard deviation) provide numerical summaries that complement visual insights. For example, while a histogram can show the distribution of a variable, the mean and standard deviation provide precise numerical descriptions of its central value and spread.

EDA also involves making initial hypotheses about the data. This is where domain knowledge becomes invaluable. Understanding the context and background of the data allows you to generate meaningful hypotheses and test them using statistical methods. For instance, if you are analyzing sales data, you might hypothesize that certain products sell better during specific times of the year. You can test this hypothesis by examining sales trends over time.

Anomalies and outliers can significantly impact the results of data analysis, making their detection and treatment a critical part of EDA. Outliers can be identified using visualizations like box plots or statistical methods such as the Z-score or the Interquartile Range (IQR) method. Once identified, decisions must be made about how to handle them. Options include removing outliers, transforming them, or investigating them further to understand why they occur.

It's also important to consider the quality of the data. Data quality issues such as inconsistencies, inaccuracies, and biases can affect the reliability of the analysis. Data profiling is a technique used to assess the data's quality by examining its characteristics and identifying potential issues. This process involves checking for consistency, accuracy, completeness, and validity of the data.

EDA is an iterative process. It often involves going back and forth between different steps as new insights are uncovered. For instance, after visualizing the data, you might discover anomalies that require further cleaning or transformation. Similarly, initial hypotheses might need to be refined or revised based on the findings from the exploratory analysis.

In practice, documenting the EDA process is crucial. Keeping a record of the steps taken, the decisions made, and the insights gained helps in maintaining transparency and reproducibility. This documentation can be in the form of code comments, Jupyter notebooks, or detailed reports. It ensures that the process can be reviewed and understood by others, facilitating collaboration and future analysis.

In summary, EDA is a fundamental step in the data analysis process that provides a deep understanding of the data. It involves a combination of data cleaning, visualization, summary statistics, and hypothesis testing. By thoroughly exploring the data, you can uncover patterns, detect anomalies, and gain insights that guide subsequent analysis and decision-making. As you become more experienced with EDA, you'll develop an intuition for the data, allowing you to conduct more efficient and effective analyses.

This intuition will also enable you to tailor your EDA process to specific datasets and analytical goals, making your work not only more efficient but also more insightful. As you refine your EDA skills, you'll find yourself better equipped to handle complex datasets and uncover deeper insights.

Descriptive Statistics

Descriptive statistics form the bedrock of data analysis, providing a way to summarize and understand the essential features of a dataset. They transform raw data into meaningful information, enabling you to comprehend and communicate the data's structure and patterns effectively. This chapter explores the core concepts, measures, and tools of descriptive statistics, offering practical guidance for beginners to grasp and apply these fundamental techniques.

Picture a scenario where you are given a dataset containing sales figures for a retail store. Your task is to glean insights and present a clear picture of the store's performance. Diving into descriptive statistics allows you to summarize and describe the dataset succinctly, making it easier to identify trends, anomalies, and key characteristics.

The first step in descriptive statistics involves understanding the types of data you are dealing with. Data can be broadly classified into two categories: quantitative and qualitative. Quantitative data represents numerical values, such as sales amounts or customer ages, which can be further divided into discrete and continuous data. Discrete data consists of countable values, like the number of products sold, while continuous data includes measurements on a continuous scale, such as revenue. Qualitative data, on the other hand, represents categorical values, such as product categories or customer satisfaction levels.

One of the primary objectives of descriptive statistics is to summarize quantitative data using measures of central tendency and dispersion. Measures of central tendency, including the mean, median, and mode, provide a single value that represents the center of the data distribution. The mean, or average, is calculated by summing all the values and dividing by the number of observations. It is sensitive to outliers, which can skew the results. The median, the middle value when the data is ordered, is less affected by outliers and provides a better measure of central tendency for skewed distributions. The mode, the most frequently occurring value, is useful for identifying common categories in qualitative data.

Consider a dataset of daily sales figures over a month. Calculating the mean sales provides a general idea of the store's average daily revenue. However, if there were a few exceptionally high sales days, the mean might give a distorted picture. In such cases, the median sales figure offers a more accurate representation of typical daily revenue.

Measures of dispersion describe the spread or variability of the data. These include the range, variance, and standard deviation. The range is the simplest measure of dispersion, calculated as the difference between the maximum and minimum values. While easy to compute, the range can be misleading if the dataset contains outliers. Variance measures the average squared deviation of each value from the mean, providing a more comprehensive understanding of variability. The standard deviation, the square root of the variance, is in the same units as the data and is widely used to describe the spread of values around the mean.

For instance, knowing that the mean daily sales are $500 with a standard deviation of $50 indicates that most daily sales figures fall within $450 to $550. A higher standard deviation would suggest more variability and less consistency in daily sales.

When dealing with qualitative data, frequency distributions and relative frequencies are essential tools. A frequency distribution lists each category and the number of occurrences, while relative frequencies express these counts as percentages of the total. These summaries help visualize the distribution of categorical data, making it easier to identify dominant categories and patterns.

Imagine analyzing customer feedback ratings for a product. A frequency distribution might reveal that 60% of customers rated the product 5 stars, 25% gave it 4 stars, and the rest rated it 3 stars or lower. This distribution highlights the product's overall customer satisfaction and areas needing improvement.

Visualizations play a significant role in descriptive statistics, providing intuitive ways to interpret and communicate data. Histograms, bar charts, and pie charts are commonly used to depict distributions and frequencies. A histogram, for instance, displays the frequency distribution of a quantitative variable by grouping data into bins and plotting the number of observations in each bin. This visualization helps identify the shape of the distribution, such as normal, skewed, or bimodal.

Bar charts and pie charts are ideal for summarizing qualitative data. A bar chart uses rectangular bars to represent the frequency or relative frequency of categories, making it easy to compare different groups. Pie charts, on the other hand, show the proportion of each category as segments of a circle, providing a visual representation of the whole.

Suppose you are analyzing the product categories sold in a store. A bar chart could show that electronics have the highest sales, followed by clothing and home goods. A pie chart might illustrate that electronics account for 40% of total sales, clothing 30%, and home goods 20%, with the remaining categories making up the rest.

Another important aspect of descriptive statistics is the use of cross-tabulations, or contingency tables, to examine relationships between two categorical variables. These tables display the frequency distribution of variables in a matrix format, helping identify patterns and associations. For example, a cross-tabulation of customer age groups and product categories might reveal that younger customers prefer electronics, while older customers favor home goods.

While descriptive statistics provide valuable summaries, they are not without limitations. They do not infer causality or predict future outcomes. Instead, they offer a snapshot of the data's current state, serving as a foundation for further analysis. For predictive insights and causal relationships, inferential statistics and modeling techniques are required.

In practice, descriptive statistics are often the first step in data analysis. They help clean and organize data, identify trends, and set the stage for more complex analyses. For beginners, mastering these techniques is crucial for developing a solid understanding of data and its characteristics.

To illustrate the process, consider a project analyzing monthly sales data for a retail store. The first step is to load the data and examine its structure, checking for missing values and outliers. Next, calculate measures of central tendency and dispersion to summarize the sales figures. Visualize the distribution using histograms and identify any patterns or anomalies. Create frequency distributions for categorical data, such as product categories, and use bar charts and pie charts to visualize the results. Finally, use cross-tabulations to explore relationships between variables, such as customer demographics and purchasing behavior.

Throughout the process, documenting each step ensures transparency and reproducibility. Detailed notes on data cleaning, calculations, and visualizations facilitate collaboration and future analyses. It's essential to interpret the results in the context of the data, considering any limitations and potential biases.

In summary, descriptive statistics are a fundamental tool in data analysis, providing a way to summarize and understand the essential features of a dataset. By mastering measures of central tendency and dispersion, frequency distributions, and visualizations, beginners can gain valuable insights into their data and lay the groundwork for more advanced analyses. Through practical application and continuous learning, you will develop the skills needed to effectively analyze and interpret data, making informed decisions and driving meaningful outcomes.

Descriptive statistics are indispensable not only for their ability to summarize data but also for their role in data interpretation and decision-making. These statistics provide the foundational tools that enable data analysts, researchers, and business professionals to extract meaningful insights from complex datasets, facilitating more informed and strategic decisions.

Data Visualization Techniques

Data visualization techniques are essential for transforming raw data into meaningful insights through graphical representations. These techniques help communicate complex data in a clear, concise, and visually appealing manner, making it easier for audiences to understand trends, patterns, and outliers. Effective data visualization is a blend of art and science, requiring an understanding of the data, the message it conveys, and the most appropriate visual tools to use.

Imagine you're working with a dataset containing sales figures for a retail chain over several years. Your goal is to present this data to the company's executives to help them make strategic decisions. A well-crafted visualization can reveal seasonal trends, highlight the most profitable products, and identify underperforming regions at a glance. Without such visual aids, conveying this information would be much more challenging and less impactful.

One of the foundational tools in data visualization is the bar chart. Bar charts are used to compare quantities across different categories. For example, if you want to compare the sales performance of different product categories, a bar chart can effectively display each category's sales figures side by side. This visual comparison allows viewers to quickly identify which categories are performing well and which are lagging.

Another powerful technique is the line chart, which is ideal for displaying data trends over time. For instance, plotting monthly sales figures over several years in a line chart can reveal seasonal patterns, growth trends, and cyclical fluctuations. Line charts are particularly useful for identifying long-term trends and making future projections based on historical data.

Histograms are another valuable tool, particularly for understanding the distribution of a single variable. They show the frequency of data points within specified ranges, allowing you to see how data is spread out over a range of values. For example, a histogram of customer ages can reveal the most common age groups among your customer base, helping tailor marketing strategies to target these demographics more effectively.

Pie charts, though sometimes criticized for their potential to mislead, can be useful for showing proportions and percentages within a whole. They are best used when you have a limited number of categories, and the differences between them are significant. For instance, a pie chart showing the market share of different competitors in the industry can provide a quick overview of the competitive landscape.

Scatter plots are indispensable when you need to explore the relationship between two quantitative variables. By plotting data points on a Cartesian plane, scatter plots can reveal correlations, clusters, and outliers. For example, a scatter plot of advertising expenditure versus sales revenue can help determine if there is a positive correlation between the two, indicating that increased advertising leads to higher sales.

Heat maps are effective for visualizing data that is part of a matrix or grid format, showing variations across multiple dimensions. They use color gradients to represent data values, making it easy to identify areas of high and low intensity. For instance, a heat map of sales performance across different regions and product categories can quickly highlight the most profitable combinations.

Box plots, also known as box-and-whisker plots, summarize the distribution of a dataset by displaying its minimum, first quartile, median, third quartile, and maximum. They are particularly useful for identifying outliers and understanding the spread and skewness of the data. For example, a box plot of delivery times can help a logistics company identify anomalies and improve its delivery processes.

Geographical data can be effectively visualized using maps, which provide context through spatial representation. Choropleth maps, which use color shading to represent data values across geographical regions, are commonly used to display demographic information, election results, or sales performance by region. These maps can highlight regional differences and trends that might be missed in a tabular format.

Tree maps are useful for displaying hierarchical data through nested rectangles. Each branch of the hierarchy is represented by a rectangle, with the size and color of the rectangle corresponding to the data value. For example, a tree map of a company's product portfolio can show the relative contribution of each product line to the overall revenue, helping to identify key drivers of business success.

In addition to choosing the right type of visualization, it is crucial to consider the design elements that enhance clarity and readability. Using colors effectively can help differentiate data series and highlight important information. However, it's essential to use color schemes that are accessible to colorblind individuals, ensuring that everyone can interpret the data correctly.

Labels and annotations are also critical for effective data visualization. They provide context and explanations for the data points, making it easier for viewers to understand the significance of the visualized information. For example, annotating a spike in sales on a line chart with the corresponding marketing campaign can help viewers correlate the two events.

Interactive visualizations have become increasingly popular, allowing users to explore data in a more dynamic and engaging way. Tools like Tableau, Power BI, and D3.js enable the creation of interactive dashboards where users can filter data, drill down into details, and view different perspectives. These interactive elements make data exploration more intuitive and accessible, fostering better decision-making.

When creating data visualizations, it's essential to keep the audience in mind. Different stakeholders may have varying levels of data literacy and interests. Tailoring the complexity and detail of the visualization to the audience's needs ensures that the message is effectively communicated. For instance, executives might prefer high-level summaries and key insights, while data analysts might require more detailed and granular visualizations.

Storytelling is a powerful technique that can enhance the impact of data visualizations. By crafting a narrative around the data, you can guide the audience through the insights, making the information more relatable and memorable. For example, telling the story of a product's growth journey through a series of visualizations that highlight key milestones, challenges, and successes can make a more compelling case for strategic decisions.

The importance of data quality cannot be overstated in the context of data visualization. Inaccurate or incomplete data can lead to misleading visualizations and erroneous conclusions. Ensuring data integrity through proper cleaning, validation, and preprocessing is a critical step before creating any visualization. This process involves checking for missing values, outliers, and inconsistencies, and making necessary corrections to maintain the accuracy of the visualized information.

In practice, creating effective data visualizations often involves an iterative process. Starting with a draft visualization, you can refine it based on feedback and further analysis. This iterative approach helps in fine-tuning the design, improving clarity, and ensuring that the visualization effectively communicates the intended message. Collaboration with colleagues and stakeholders can provide valuable insights and perspectives, leading to more robust and impactful visualizations.

While data visualization techniques are powerful tools for data analysis and communication, they must be used responsibly. Ethical considerations, such as avoiding misleading representations and ensuring transparency, are paramount. For example, manipulating the axis scales or cherry-picking data points to support a particular narrative can lead to biased interpretations and undermine the credibility of the analysis.

Data visualization is both an art and a science, requiring a balance of technical skills and creative design. By mastering various visualization techniques and understanding their appropriate contexts, you can transform complex data into clear, insightful, and compelling stories. Whether you're presenting to executives, collaborating with colleagues, or communicating with a broader audience, effective data visualization can significantly enhance your ability to convey data-driven insights and drive informed decision-making. Through continuous learning and practice, you can develop the expertise to create visualizations that not only inform but also inspire action and drive meaningful outcomes.

Effective data visualization also hinges on understanding the principles of design and human perception. One fundamental principle is the use of visual hierarchy to guide the viewer's eye to the most important information first. This can be achieved through the strategic use of size, color, and positioning. For example, a larger font size or a bolder color can draw attention to key metrics, while less critical information can be de-emphasized.

Identifying Patterns and Trends

Recognizing patterns and trends in data is a fundamental skill for anyone looking to make informed decisions based on data analysis. Patterns represent regularities or structured repetitions in data, while trends indicate directions in which data points move over time. Identifying these elements can reveal crucial insights, drive strategy, and uncover opportunities that might not be obvious at first glance.

Imagine you are tasked with analyzing sales data for a retail company over the past five years. At a glance, the raw numbers may seem overwhelming. However, by identifying patterns and trends within this data, you can extract valuable insights that inform strategic decisions. For example, you might notice that certain products sell better during specific seasons, or that there is a gradual increase in sales following a particular marketing campaign. These observations can help in planning inventory, marketing strategies, and resource allocation.

One effective way to start identifying patterns is through visualizations such as line charts, bar charts, and heat maps. Line charts are particularly useful for observing trends over time. By plotting sales data on a line chart, you can easily see the rise and fall of sales across different periods. This visual representation can highlight seasonal trends, such as increased sales during the holiday season, as well as long-term trends, like steady growth or decline.

Heat maps can show you patterns across different dimensions. For example, a heat map of sales data across various regions and product categories might reveal that certain regions consistently outperform others, or that specific product categories are more popular in particular areas. This type of visualization uses color gradients to represent data values, making it easy to spot areas of high and low intensity.

Histograms are another useful tool, especially when you need to understand the distribution of a single variable. For instance, a histogram of customer ages can show the most common age groups among your customer base. This information is invaluable for tailoring marketing strategies and product offerings to target these demographic segments effectively.

Moving beyond visualizations, statistical methods such as moving averages and regression analysis can help identify trends. A moving average smooths out short-term fluctuations and highlights longer-term trends. This method is particularly useful when dealing with time series data that exhibits a lot of volatility. For example, applying a moving average to daily sales data can help you see the underlying trend without the noise of daily fluctuations.

Regression analysis, on the other hand, can help determine the strength and nature of relationships between variables. By fitting a regression line to your data, you can quantify the relationship between sales and factors like marketing spend, price changes, or economic indicators. This analysis can reveal whether increases in marketing budget are associated with higher sales, or if changes in pricing strategy correlate with shifts in consumer demand.

Another effective approach is clustering, which involves grouping data points that exhibit similar characteristics. Clustering can uncover hidden patterns within your data. For example, clustering customer data based on purchasing behavior can help identify distinct customer segments. These segments can then be targeted with personalized marketing campaigns, improving the effectiveness of your outreach efforts.

Seasonal decomposition is a technique used to separate a time series into its seasonal, trend, and residual components. This method is particularly useful for identifying patterns in data that exhibit regular seasonal variations. By decomposing sales data, you can isolate the seasonal component to understand how much of the variation is due to seasonal factors, and how much is due to underlying trends or irregularities.

In practice, identifying patterns and trends also involves a healthy dose of domain knowledge. Understanding the context in which the data was collected and the business environment can provide critical insights that pure statistical methods might miss. For instance, a sudden spike in sales might be attributed to an external event like a competitor going out of business or a new product launch. Without this contextual knowledge, you might misinterpret the data.

It's also important to be aware of potential pitfalls when identifying patterns and trends. One common issue is overfitting, where a model becomes too complex and starts to capture noise rather than the underlying pattern. Overfitting can lead to misleading conclusions and poor predictive performance. To mitigate this risk, it's essential to validate your models using out-of-sample data or cross-validation techniques.

Another challenge is the presence of outliers, which are data points that deviate significantly from the rest of the dataset. Outliers can distort your analysis and obscure genuine patterns. Identifying and addressing outliers, either by investigating their causes or using robust statistical methods that minimize their impact, is crucial for accurate trend analysis.

When working with large datasets, automation and advanced analytics tools can be incredibly beneficial. Software like Tableau, Power BI, and Python libraries like pandas and scikit-learn offer powerful functionalities for pattern and trend analysis. These tools can handle large volumes of data, apply sophisticated algorithms, and generate interactive visualizations that make it easier to spot patterns and trends.

Consider the example of a marketing analyst working for an e-commerce platform. By leveraging these tools, the analyst can automate the process of generating weekly sales reports, apply clustering algorithms to segment customers, and use regression analysis to evaluate the impact of different marketing campaigns. This automation not only saves time but also ensures consistency and accuracy in the analysis.

In addition to technical skills, effective communication is essential for conveying the insights derived from pattern and trend analysis. This involves creating clear and compelling visualizations, crafting narratives that explain the findings, and tailoring the presentation to the audience's level of expertise. For instance, a detailed statistical analysis might be appropriate for a technical audience, while a high-level summary with key takeaways would be more suitable for senior executives.

Storytelling can play a powerful role in this context. By framing data insights within a narrative, you can make the information more relatable and memorable.

For example, instead of simply presenting a trend line showing increased sales, you can tell the story of how a new marketing strategy led to a surge in customer engagement and sales growth. This approach not only highlights the data but also connects it to real-world actions and outcomes.

Ethical considerations are paramount when identifying and presenting patterns and trends. Ensuring data accuracy, avoiding manipulation or misrepresentation of data, and being transparent about the limitations of your analysis are all critical components of ethical data practice. Misleading visualizations or selective reporting can have serious consequences, from misinformed business decisions to loss of trust.

In summary, identifying patterns and trends in data requires a combination of visualization techniques, statistical methods, domain knowledge, and effective communication skills. By leveraging these tools and approaches, you can transform raw data into actionable insights that drive informed decision-making and strategic planning. Whether you are analyzing sales data, customer behavior, or market trends, the ability to recognize and interpret patterns and trends is a valuable skill that can provide a competitive edge in today's data-driven world.

Moreover, as you delve deeper into the realm of pattern and trend analysis, you'll find that the ability to predict future outcomes becomes increasingly valuable. Predictive analytics leverages historical data to forecast future events, enabling proactive decision-making. Techniques such as time series forecasting, machine learning, and advanced statistical modeling are pivotal in this regard.

Case Studies in EDA

One of the most effective ways to understand exploratory data analysis (EDA) is through real-world case studies. These case studies provide concrete examples of how EDA can be applied to uncover insights, identify patterns, and inform decision-making across various domains. Each case study presents unique challenges and demonstrates different techniques and tools used in the EDA process. By examining these examples, beginners can gain practical knowledge and inspiration for their own data analysis projects.

Imagine a scenario where a healthcare organization wants to analyze patient data to improve treatment outcomes. The dataset includes patient demographics, medical histories, treatment plans, and outcomes. The first step in EDA for this case would be to understand the structure of the data. This involves examining the types of variables, their distributions, and any missing values. Visualizations such as histograms and box plots can be useful here, providing a clear picture of the data distribution and highlighting any outliers or anomalies.

Next, the analysts might explore relationships between different variables. For instance, they could use scatter plots to examine the correlation between age and treatment outcomes, or bar charts to compare the success rates of different treatment plans. These visualizations can reveal patterns and trends that might not be immediately obvious from the raw data. For example, the analysis might show that younger patients tend to have better outcomes, or that a particular treatment plan is more effective for patients with certain medical histories.

In another case study, consider a retail company looking to optimize its inventory management. The dataset includes sales data, product details, and inventory levels. The EDA process begins with a thorough examination of the sales data to identify any seasonal trends or patterns. Line charts can be particularly useful for this purpose, showing how sales fluctuate over time. By overlaying sales data with inventory levels, the analysts can identify periods of overstocking or stockouts, which can inform future inventory planning.

Cluster analysis is another powerful technique that can be applied in this context. By clustering products based on sales patterns, the company can identify groups of products that behave similarly. For example, some products might have consistent sales throughout the year, while others might be highly seasonal. These insights can help the company develop more targeted inventory strategies, ensuring that high-demand products are always in stock while minimizing excess inventory for seasonal items.

A more complex case study involves a financial institution analyzing transaction data to detect fraudulent activities. The dataset includes transaction details such as amounts, dates, locations, and account information. The first step in EDA for this case is to understand the typical behavior of legitimate transactions. This involves calculating summary statistics such as mean, median, and standard deviation for transaction amounts, and creating visualizations like density plots to understand the distribution of transaction amounts.

Next, the analysts might explore the relationships between different variables to identify any unusual patterns. For example, they could use heat maps to examine the frequency of transactions across different times of the day or days of the week. By comparing these patterns with known fraudulent transactions, they can develop a better understanding of what constitutes suspicious behavior. Techniques such as anomaly detection can then be applied to flag transactions that deviate significantly from the norm.

In another example, a social media company might use EDA to analyze user engagement data. The dataset includes metrics such as the number of likes, shares, comments, and post views. The EDA process starts with a basic examination of these metrics to understand their distributions and identify any outliers. For instance, a box plot of the number of likes per post can reveal whether there are any posts with unusually high or low engagement.

Correlation analysis can also be useful in this context, helping to identify relationships between different engagement metrics. For example, a scatter plot might show a strong positive correlation between the number of shares and the number of comments, suggesting that posts that are frequently shared also tend to generate more discussion. These insights can help the company develop strategies to boost user engagement, such as promoting content that is likely to be shared widely.

In the context of a manufacturing company, EDA can be applied to analyze production data and improve operational efficiency. The dataset might include information on production volumes, machine performance, and defect rates. The EDA process begins with an examination of summary statistics to understand the overall performance of the production process. For example, calculating the mean and standard deviation of production volumes can provide insights into the consistency of the manufacturing process.

Next, the analysts might explore relationships between different variables to identify factors that influence production efficiency. For instance, they could use scatter plots to examine the relationship between machine performance metrics and defect rates. If a particular machine shows a high defect rate, further analysis might reveal underlying issues such as maintenance needs or operator errors. These insights can inform targeted interventions to improve production efficiency and reduce defect rates.

In another case study, a transportation company might use EDA to analyze fleet performance data. The dataset includes metrics such as fuel consumption, maintenance records, and vehicle utilization rates. The first step in EDA is to understand the distribution of these metrics, using visualizations such as histograms and box plots. For example, a histogram of fuel consumption can reveal whether there are any vehicles that consume significantly more fuel than others.

The analysts might then explore relationships between different variables to identify factors that impact fleet performance. For instance, they could use correlation analysis to examine the relationship between maintenance frequency and vehicle utilization rates. If vehicles with more frequent maintenance show higher utilization rates, this might suggest that regular maintenance helps to improve vehicle reliability and performance. These insights can inform fleet management strategies, such as optimizing maintenance schedules to maximize vehicle uptime.

In all these case studies, the EDA process involves a combination of data visualization, summary statistics, and correlation analysis to uncover insights and inform decision-making. The specific techniques and tools used can vary depending on the nature of the data and the goals of the analysis. However, the overarching principles remain the same: understanding the data structure, identifying patterns and relationships, and using these insights to drive informed decisions.

EDA is not a one-size-fits-all approach; it requires a flexible and iterative mindset. As new data becomes available, analysts must be prepared to revisit their analysis, refine their techniques, and explore new perspectives. By continuously applying EDA, organizations can stay ahead of trends, respond to emerging challenges, and capitalize on new opportunities. These case studies illustrate the power of EDA in transforming raw data into actionable insights, providing a foundation for data-driven decision-making across diverse domains.

Another compelling case study involves a non-profit organization aiming to analyze donor data to enhance fundraising efforts. The dataset includes donor demographics, donation amounts, donation frequency, and campaign details. The initial step in EDA for this scenario involves understanding the donor base. Analysts might start by examining the distribution of donation amounts using histograms and analyzing donor demographics with pie charts or bar graphs. This helps in identifying the most common donation amounts and the predominant demographics of the donor base.